Not Alone

Not Alone

Reflections on Faith and Depression

A 40-Day Devotional

Monica A. Coleman

Inner Prizes, Inc.
PO Box 122
Culver City, CA 90232
www.innerprizes.com

softcover ISBN: 978-0-9851402-0-5
ebook ISBN: 978-0-9851402-1-2

Cover design by Brad Norr
Interior design by Beth Wright, Trio Bookworks, triobookworks.com
Author photo by Anne Almasy, www.annealmasy.com

To all who let me know that my public writing mattered
To all who are looking for a co-journeyer . . .
YOU ARE NOT ALONE
To God be the glory

Contents

Letting Others In

Touching Love, Beauty, and Joy

Knowing Yourself as Complete and Whole

Embracing Death as a New Beginning

introduction

I began blogging about faith and depression in 2010 at www.BeautifulMindBlog.com, as an outgrowth of conversations I had with a good friend. We are both people of faith. We are both religious scholars. We both live with depressive conditions. And we both yearned to read about our own experiences of wrestling with our faith while living with debilitating sadness.

I started writing about my own experiences to rid myself of the shame that came from hiding my depressions from most of the people around me. I also wanted to show how a minister and theologian struggles with faith in the midst of living with a depressive condition: I yell at God; I believe some scriptures are lies; I grow impatient; I find holiness in new places; I create rituals; I lean on God. I lay bare my greatest fears, frustrations, and lessons as I encounter each day—happy or sad.

In the fall of 2011, I received this email:

> I am currently in an inpatient psychiatric program for severe depression. I'm learning a lot about what it means to live with this illness and I am frequently scared. Your posts make it seem like I'm *not alone*.

This book is for the person who wrote this email.

This book is for people of faith.

This book is for people who live with depression.

This book is for people who live with bipolar depression.

This book is for those who are willing to walk inside a winding journey.

This book is for those who resist easy answers.

This book is for those who are willing to go deeper.

This book is to let us know that we are not alone.

We are not alone in our sadness. We are not alone in our silence. We are not alone in our tears. We are not alone in our faith.

This book is an invitation to explore and reflect. It is presented as a forty-day devotional. In Jewish and Christian traditions, the number forty represents a time of waiting and of preparation. Many significant stories of faith reflect the number forty:

- In Noah's time, the rains fell for forty days and nights.
- The Hebrew people were in the wilderness with manna from God for forty years.
- Moses was with God on the mountain for forty days and nights.
- David was king of Israel for forty years.
- Jesus fasted for forty days and nights.
- Jesus was tempted in the wilderness for forty days.
- The risen Jesus was on the earth for forty days before the ascension.

These are some of the reasons why the Christian liturgical season of Lent lasts for forty days. You may choose to read this during a season like Lent or at any other time. Like the forty days in Jewish and Christian traditions, the forty days you spend with these devotions can be a time of preparation. It is meant to be a time when you are willing to explore and reflect on your own experiences and your faith. It should be a time when you are willing to be honest with yourself and God. It should be a time when you are open to experiencing holiness in new ways.

The devotions are grouped into six sections that loosely correspond to what I'm learning in my journey with faith and depression. I've learned these lessons through engaging holy texts and stories in Jewish and Christian traditions, but also through my encounters with culture, family, music, film, community, and other religious traditions.

Breaking the Silence represents the phase of coming to one's own terms with a depressive condition. It's about shirking shame, telling the truth, naming yourself, and singing your own song.

Feeling It Deeply discusses some of the experiences of living with a depressive condition. It's about feeling impatient, broken, empty, lost, quiet, and desperate. It's also about feeling full, heroic, and grounded. Sometimes it's about not feeling anything at all.

Letting Others In reflects my sense that we cannot travel this journey alone. We all must have someone or some ones. This section is about looking, walking, moving, eating, connecting, communicating, creating, and even resting with others—and inviting them to do the same with us.

Touching Love, Beauty, and Joy is a reminder that living with a depressive condition is not all sadness. In the ordinary moments of our lives, there can be joy, laughter, happiness, and gratitude.

Knowing Yourself as Complete and Whole talks about how messy wellness really is. We heal as we amble through desire, rest, memory, medication, affirmation, language, new skills, and new rituals.

Embracing Death as a New Beginning grapples with the tension between looking back and moving forward. This section is about the search for peace and comfort. It's about holding on tightly and the need to mourn, let go, and take flight in our lives. I've ended these reflections with an epilogue about why I've found that resurrection matters so much—because of the encounter of depression and faith.

Each devotion is followed by two questions. One question invites you to explore where you have been and how you have felt. The second question invites you to reflect on where you would like to go and how you will continue to live. I invite you to write down your answers to these questions. You might choose to do this in your own journal. You may find a partner or small group with whom to reflect on this book—or you may be content to do this during the quiet moments of your life. There are no right or wrong answers. You may not even be able to answer some of these questions at this time. In fact, you may come back to this devotional again and have different answers than before. These differences simply reflect the changes that take place in all of our lives and the thoughts you have at that particular time.

I've shared some of my experiences in hopes that you find some resonance here. May this exploration of faith and depression remind you that the questioning, hoping, desiring, waiting, and feeling (or lack of feeling) is part of the process. You are not alone.

—*Monica A. Coleman*
Los Angeles, CA
February 2012

Breaking
the Silence

a closet of my own

I was still in high school when *Essence* magazine published an article by its then editor Linda Villarosa and her mother, Clara Villarosa. "Coming Out" told the story of Linda's revelation and acceptance of her lesbian identity—from her perspective and from her mother's perspective. This story stayed with me because it was the first time I heard about "the closet." Although new to me at the time, the closet is a common metaphor for describing the ways that lesbians and gays hide or deny their sexualities from the wider world around them. In the article, Linda Villarosa writes, "I tried to straddle both worlds, happy with my lover and pretending to be accepting of my new life, but secretly scared and insecure. . . . I was passing but always petrified that someone would uncover my secret."

As a teenager, I could not have explained why I found this article so compelling, or why I related so closely to Linda's description of the closet. But I was living in a closet of my own. I knew how it felt to be happy and free in some contexts, and terrified and alone in others. I now realize that I have known this feeling for most of my life. I have lived with long and terrible depressions since I was a teenager. And this was my secret.

I was convinced that even if I looked happy and successful on the outside, that if people dug just a little deeper, they would find a river of sadness flowing just below the surface of my skin. I worked hard to keep people from touching me below my joyful epidermis. At times this took all the energy I could muster. Other times, it was easier because I actually felt happy. I received such affirmation for my professional successes and my effervescent personality that I came to believe that this was the part of me that people loved—the only part of me that people loved. If people knew who I really was, how sad I really was, they would not love me. I wanted to be loved, so I had to hide. Inside a closet of my own.

For years, I lacked a language for my condition. The constant moving associated with my education and employment meant that I was rarely in the same place for long: I had new doctors, new friends, and a new community every couple of years. Few people knew me long enough to see the deep sorrow *and* the long bursts of energy and productivity that produced my résumé. Few people knew me well enough to see this. I did not let them. And like a river shored up by a shoddily made dam, my condition leaked through the gaping holes in my life. Those with eyes to see—usually lovers, and friends who were therapists—began to ask me about my depression.

"What depression?" I replied.

I never admitted my deep, constant levels of pain until I was raped. Therapy and research taught me that I was responding to the trauma of rape. I owned the suffering and the healing process. I became an activist against sexual violence, hiding the fact that I had nightmares and tears long before I was raped—and long after. Two significant suicidal episodes, medication, and hospitalization did not remove the shame I felt about living with what my doctors would name Bipolar II. And yet, as Audre Lorde wrote so poignantly, "my silences had not protected me." Depression is a part of my life whether I tell anyone or not, whether I hide or not.

I'm terrified. I am afraid of being called "crazy." I am an academic. I make my living off of my mind, and my mind can play deathly tricks on me. I am a minister. I tell people that God loves them and wants the best for them. The truth is that depression can make you question everything—especially whether God loves you. I am a sister, daughter, cousin, niece, lover, colleague, friend, and other-mother. Will these people still love me when they learn that I've been lying to them about who I am and how I feel? The fact that I've spoken out against sexual violence for almost fifteen years does not make this any easier. Rape was a discrete event that someone else did to me. Living with levels of debilitating sadness comes from inside of me. I can't name a beginning or an end. It is with me. I am mortally afraid of talking about this.

Yet I will. Because I know what it's like to search for metaphors, stories, and narratives to give voice to what seems so wordless inside. I've read newsletters, blogs, memoirs, and textbooks looking for someone to describe how this feels. And for what it's like to be faithful in the midst of these feelings.

I met Linda Villarosa in 2006, when I invited her to speak at a conference on black women, mental health, and faith at Bennett College for Women. I told her that I remembered her 1991 article. I told her how it spoke to me. I told her about my closet. During that conference, I came out. Huddling away from the spring rains in the historic chapel, the audience heard me say that I lived with a depressive condition. The ground did not open and swallow me up. There were no loud gasps coming from the audience. No one threw tomatoes at me. I did not die.

I am not alone. I have a quiet community of friends who live with different types of clinical depressions. Dispersed around the country and at first unknown to one another, we discovered our bond only when one of us let it slip in intimate conversation. Now we know from the first "hello" if something is wrong. We sit and lose time together. We check in on one another. We talk about medication, exercise, and sunshine. We know when to become officially worried.

So I'm ranting and writing for us, and for the people who know us and love us. Because, as Linda wrote in her article, "The closet is dark and lonely and not someplace I plan to hide away."

∽

Exploration
How do you hide?

Reflection
What scares you the most about sharing?

the power of honesty

I have a couple of confessions: I like soap operas. Not all, but a couple. I've been following their story lines for years. At the end of almost every weekday, I indulge myself by watching the day's episode online. It seems like a perfectly mindless way to unwind. I jokingly tell friends, "Whatever's going on in my life, it will pale in comparison to the drama these characters invoke in their lives." I know it's TV. I know it's not real. Yet the philosopher in me is fascinated by how years of television can operate off of two basic axioms: (1) I can make so-and-so love me, and (2) it's better if I don't tell so-and-so the truth. I'm convinced that these two principles have been the core of dramatic storytelling for decades.

The second axiom fascinates me because it so clearly contradicts the oft-cited biblical passage "The truth shall set you free."

The context of this passage complicates this statement. Jesus is teaching the crowds in the temple. He's talking about sin and death and his relationship to the world. Speaking to the believers, Jesus says, "If you continue in my word, you are truly my disciples; and you will know the truth, and the truth will make you free" (John 8:31-32).

As an educator committed to social transformation, I'm delighted by the way Jesus connects his teachings to community, knowledge, and liberation. I read this passage and see that communities can come together around spiritual teachings and feel secure in their knowledge of God. I understand how intimacy with God can grant a sense of liberty.

But most of us simply pull this verse out of context: "The truth shall set you free."

Translation: "Don't lie. It's better that way."

I want to think I'm aligned with this biblical principle. Nevertheless, I am one of many people who find themselves drawn to a particular scene from the movie *A Few Good Men*. It takes place in a military court of law; Tom Cruise plays Lt. Daniel Kaffee, the lead counsel for the defense. Questioning Col. Nathan Jessup, played by the inimitable Jack Nicholson, Cruise's character yells, "I want the truth!" Nicholson delivers the well-known line in response, "YOU CAN'T HANDLE THE TRUTH!"

I often believe more in the words of Jack Nicholson than in the inspirational words of the Gospel of John. That's confession number two. And I don't think I'm alone.

As someone who lives with depression, I have a tenuous relationship with the truth. I know that depression can make me believe things that aren't factually true. Things like this: no one loves me; no one really knows me; no one sees who I really am. Depression can turn my deepest insecurities into facts that can overwhelm me to the point of emotional paralysis.

As a fairly functional depressive (and one who has been closeted more often than not), I also know how to lie. I know how to work and teach and preach as if I'm okay. I know how to contain the tears and shivering to my private moments alone at night. I know how to fake it until I make it. I can do this for months, years even, before most people know how miserable I am. I don't recommend this. It is exhausting and lonely.

But down deep, I admit I've embraced Jack Nicholson's approach more than Jesus' words. I didn't think people around me could handle my truth. I've believed that my colleagues and superiors wouldn't respect me if they knew about my struggles and vulnerabilities. They would not hire me. They would not promote me. I've believed that people closest to me needed me to be strong and "together." I've believed that my friends would not love me if they knew how sad I really was.

I told myself that this was the lesser of many evils because I never lied to myself. I knew how poorly I felt. I knew when I slid from something-I-can-manage to I-better-find-a-doctor-quickly. I thought my self-awareness was honesty. I've always told doctors what was going on.

I understand that this is a rarity. On the television show *House*, the expert medical diagnostician Dr. Gregory House says, "People always lie." By this, he means that patients do not tell the full truth about their lives and symptoms, thereby rendering it even more difficult for doctors to make an accurate diagnosis. Dr. House feels this so strongly that he insists that the doctors he supervises break into the homes of their patients in search of more information.

It's an extreme position, but I suspect many doctors are trained like House. They are trained to believe that patients are not telling the whole story. They don't say, "Everybody lies." Rather, sometimes doctors are trained to pay more attention to symptoms than to what the patient says.

But people who live with depressive conditions can't depend on someone to pay attention to their "symptoms." We have to tell someone. We have to tell someone how we really feel and what's happening, so that they can help us. Most of us cannot wait until someone else notices, or we'll be far down a road from which some people don't return.

Those of us who are reticent about telling the truth about our depressions may be as insecure as I can be. They may be wisely attuned to the stigma of mental health challenges and how prejudice can adversely affect one's ability to make a living. Other people believe that acknowledgment of depression is tantamount to admitting defeat. I can understand that as well.

Some spiritual, philosophical, and psychological systems believe in affirmations. They believe that we can tell ourselves things that are not true, things that we want to be true, or even things that we hold to be true, even when we don't feel them. We do this in order to encourage ourselves to live into them. We do this to retrain our brains, minds, and consciousnesses to conform to these ideas. I believe there is power in such a system. I believe there is power in learning to live into our highest, most godly selves.

But the power is lost when we do so at the risk of lying to ourselves, to the people closest to us, or to the people who could help us.

My truth is not usually pretty. On any given day, it could be: I'm unhappy; I didn't sleep well; I lost my appetite three weeks ago; I'm not really sure if you love me; I miss my friends; and no, I don't think if I try again tomorrow, it will be better.

These are the kinds of things I tend to keep to myself.

Each day I fight the Jack Nicholson in me in favor of Jesus' words about truth and freedom. My closest friends are like Jesus' disciples: they are my community; they can handle my truth; they hold my hand as we journey toward a land of liberty. They remind me that telling the truth is not just a biblical commandment I have to follow to get to a good place. Rather, it's one of the most powerful gifts I can give myself and those I love.

Exploration
What is your ugliest truth?

Reflection
Who in your life can handle the truth of how you feel?

words matter

"Sticks and stones may break my bones, but words will never hurt me." This is one of the biggest playground lies. The truth is that words *do* matter. Names matter. It matters what we call ourselves. What other people call us matters. And words stick with us for longer than the time it takes to heal from a physical injury.

Crazy. Manic. Depressed. Sad. Blue. High. Anxious. Psychotic. Hypersexual. Certifiable.

Most people have some idea of what these words mean. They've made their way into common parlance. We hear these words on TV; we see these words in advertisements for medication; we use these words ourselves, often in casual, usually imprecise ways.

But these words mean something particular to experts. Experts are working on the fifth edition of the *Diagnostic and Statistical Manual of Mental Disorders* (abbreviated DSM), the psychiatrist's encyclopedia, which names and classifies mental health challenges. It clusters symptoms and names them, thereby indicating who is normal and who is not. And I'm not sure if this is a good or a bad thing.

Having a name can help. It can reassure you that you are neither alone nor peculiar. There are others who experience something like what you experience. And if that experience causes deep suffering and widens the door to death, there can be help. Naming mental health conditions helps doctors know what medications may help and what medications will only make it worse. Naming mental health conditions can provide more opportunities for educational or governmental assistance when it's needed.

But there's also a danger. With the way medical and life insurance is currently structured, naming mental health conditions can raise premiums or cause someone to be denied treatments that are desperately needed. (The Wellstone-Domenici Act instituted mental health parity laws, but it still doesn't apply to individual health insurance and Medicaid.)

Moreover, as Dr. Michael First of Columbia University reminds us, naming mental health conditions can become a system of labeling that increases the stigma people experience. I also wonder about what happens to children who are diagnosed. I believe that some will experience greater health. They will receive appropriate treatment and care, which they might not have received without a diagnosis. And yet I wonder how many children will be labeled and medicated who in other circumstances might be considered eccentric, bright, and idiosyncratic.

Years ago I went to a local support group of a national advocacy organization. As the meeting began, we were asked to introduce ourselves. Everyone went around the room saying their first name and the DSM classification of their challenge. "Hi, my name is Monica, and I have . . ." I felt as if I were trapped in a late-night television spoof of Alcoholics Anonymous. Were we confessing a deep, dark secret? Were we ashamed to give our full identity? Even worse, were people reducing their lives to their diagnoses?

A reduced life doesn't work for me. My diagnosis is just shorthand and not my fully developed story. It's only a very brief way of explaining some of what I live with. It's probably most helpful for psychiatrists. Mental health conditions are as unique as the people who live with them. I have two good friends with the same diagnosis, and we have pretty different experiences of depression and hypomania. More importantly, my diagnosis is just one part of what can be said about me. There's a lot more to me than this name. This name was given to me by people who write manuals.

It matters more what we name ourselves. The African American holiday of Kwanzaa highlights the principle of Kujichagulia, or self-determination. This principle reminds African Americans of how important it is "to define ourselves, name ourselves, create for ourselves, and speak for ourselves instead of being defined, named, created for and spoken for by others." Proverbs 22:1a puts it this way, "A good name is rather to be chosen than great riches."

Should we embrace or reject the labels we are assigned? Should we rejoice when there are more labels for ourselves and our children? Or should we resist them instead? Sometimes they are helpful; they are useful shorthand. Indicating my gender, race, culture, class, and sexual orientation is an abbreviated way of signaling some things about me. But they are only very general descriptions.

I am more than any one incident that happens to me. I am more than one set of experiences I have. I am more than my sadness. And yes, I am even more than my happiness. We all are.

There is value in this struggle over words. My friend and colleague Layli Phillips Maparyan writes, "Self-labeling is a psychologically and politically valuable process, yet labels and identities are socially negotiated through dialogue. People may or may not agree about how to name a thing, but the process of negotiating the label is healthy and inevitable."

In my ideal world, a doctor offers a name, explains the process of getting there, and then asks, "What would you call this? What is your name for yourself?" Together we decide—and we may decide on more than one name.

Ultimately, the revision of the DSM reminds us that medicine is a practice. It's the experts' best estimation, given the evidence in front of them. Sometimes they get it wrong, and the effects can be disastrous. But they try again, to get as close to right as possible. And when they get it right, they can save lives.

~

Exploration
What do you call your experience?

Reflection
What are some of the names that help describe who you are?

i need spirituals

Music is an important part of my life. Whether jamming to an up-beat rock song at the gym or playing a sad song incessantly after heartbreak, I, like many other people, can imagine creating a soundtrack to my life filled with the music of my generation. Music gives me the words I can't find, and it gives me a rhythm to dance or slowly rock to.

I like many different kinds of music, and I see God in a lot of it. With a thin line between the sacred and the secular, I find as much divinity in Gavin DeGraw's "I Don't Want to Be" and Martina McBride's "In My Daughter's Eyes," as I do in Kirk Franklin's "Hold Me Now." In fact, I play Michael W. Smith's version of "Breathe" before each class I teach. It centers me and reminds me that the task of training ministers, justice workers, and religious scholars is more about God than about our brains. Yes, all this from a six-minute song.

In fact, it's probably the music that constitutes my strong attachment to black churches. I was raised in black Baptist and Methodist churches populated by people raised in the South. With my mind's eye, I can still see the deacons in their plain black suits and ties sitting single file across the front row with curved spines rocking back and forth. To their right are the deaconesses in their white dresses, white hats, and white shoes, sitting proudly with straight backs and gloved hands. Intoning together in low voices, everyone sounds like altos and tenors.

Peering around the heads in front of me, I kneeled in the pews of Shiloh Baptist Church in Washington, DC (my parents' home church), trying to get a better glimpse of the singing in the front. My mother didn't pull me to my seat; she was swaying herself.

> *Wade in the water.*
> *Wade in the water, children.*
> *Waaaaaade in the water.*
> *God's gonna trouble the waters.*

While I appreciate a good hymn, gospel music, and contemporary Christian music, my earliest memories of church include the harmonious a cappella moaning birthed in the sharecropping cotton and tobacco fields of Georgia and the Carolinas.

Spirituals are such a part of my life that I'm still realizing which songs are spirituals. "Every Time I Feel the Spirit" and "Ezekiel Saw the Wheel" are songs I learned in Vacation Bible School. I assumed all little Christian kids did. In my participation in contemporary worship and predominantly white churches, I realize how particularized my religious experiences are.

The further I'm away from Southern black churches, and the more I understand depressions, the more I need spirituals. Created by enslaved Africans in the United States, spirituals express both suffering and dependence on faith. Indigenous to the African American slave experience in the United States, spirituals are the Psalter of my people—expressing rage, despondency, hope, and joy to God. Like the Psalms of the ancient Hebrew community, the slaves took their emotions to God, putting them to music and singing them in the secret hush arbors of their religious gatherings, while working and marching, and as lullabies to their children at night. Many scholars have argued that spirituals even served an insurrectionary role by encoding the paths to freedom in ways that slave masters could not understand. And, as James Cone argues in *The Spirituals and the Blues*, the spirituals are theological because "they tell us about the divine Spirit that moves the people toward unity and self-determination." The spirituals moved slaves from suffering through to God and to release. Perhaps only music can do this.

The spirituals give me a way to be sad without being alone. Because they are sung in community, they say: *It's okay to suffer. We know how you feel. We are suffering too. We all are.*

They aren't afraid to linger in the painful places. They have no need to rush to praise. They can be slow . . . drawing out one syllable over tens of seconds . . . taking their time . . . waiting. I don't dare say that enslaved Africans were living with what we now call clinical depression. I don't have the expertise or information to assert that. But they knew how to take moans, make them hums, and then turn them into words. They knew how to give voice to pain and how to do it together.

Thus I'm convinced that when Jesus cried out, "My God, My God, why have you forsaken me?" from the cross (Matthew 27:45-46), he wasn't making a profound theological statement about the hidden God. Jesus was quoting Psalm 22, the spirituals of his people. He was in pain, and he began to sing. In my sanctified imagination, I see the people at the foot of the cross joining him as we do today in my faith community: slowly at first, one voice, then another, humming, then forming words. It sounds like this:

> *Sometimes I feel like a motherless child,*
> *sometimes I feel like a motherless child,*

sometimes I feel like a motherless child,
a long way from home

When the women of Sweet Honey in the Rock sing this spiritual, they add a verse: "And I can hear my mother calling me, she's calling me." They remind me that if you stay in a spiritual long enough, you'll hear God, you'll feel hope. In the depths of depression, I can think of no greater spiritual gift.

≈

Exploration
What songs express how you feel?

Reflection
How can you linger in the hard places?

Feeling It
Deeply

(not) feeling God

I want to feel God. I don't need a mystical experience or a burning bush, but I want to feel God. I need to *feel* God.

I was taught not to depend on my feelings for God. I spent my college years as an active member of Campus Crusade for Christ. It was a wonderful experience in which I made close friends and grew in my relationship with God. As an evangelical organization, we were taught how to teach various tracts, or little booklets about Christianity, that we would pass out and share with others. One of these tracts was called "The Four Spiritual Laws." At the end of the booklet is a diagram that gives images for the relationship among faith, fact, and feeling that C. S. Lewis describes in his book *Mere Christianity.* Lewis puts it this way:

> Now Faith, in the sense in which I am here using the
> word, is the art of holding on to things your reason has
> once accepted, in spite of your changing moods. For
> moods will change, whatever view your reason takes.

The tract explains that, for Christians, the words of God are the authority for faith. Protestants often embody this in the authority of the Bible. This is "fact": "The Christian lives by faith in the trust-worthiness of God and God's words." Using the metaphor of the train, powered by its engine and with its caboose at its end, the teachings in the tract deemphasize the role of feelings. According to the tract, feelings are the results of an individual's faith and obedience; they are the train's caboose. In contrast, the train's engine is seen to be God's word as it is found in the Bible. So, according to the tract: "The train will run with or without the caboose. However, it would be useless to attempt to pull the train by the caboose. In the same way, we as Christians do not depend on feelings or emotions, but we place our faith in the trustworthiness of God and the promises of God's words."

When we consider the ways that mood and feeling waver—especially for the traditional college-age student who is the target of much of Crusade's work—this illustration is helpful in trying to ground faith in the reality of God, rather than how one might feel from one day to the next.

As a theologian, I can go on for days about the elevation of rational thought and Western logic over experiential or emotional piety. The debate between reason and piety is a long-standing tension within Christianity and between various cultural ways of under-standing religious experience. Dismissing religious feelings has a price.

But this teaching has been particularly helpful for me as one who lives with a depressive condition. I can't always trust my feel-ings. Many days, weeks even, I see all events through the opposite of rose-colored glasses. Everything seems dismal, even when it is not. I can convince myself I have no friends. I am sure that I am completely unlovable. Nothing seems to go my way. This is not based in evidence. In fact, evidence to the contrary can usually be found without much effort. But I don't *feel* loved. I don't *feel* secure. I don't *feel* successful. I feel alone.

So I don't depend on feelings in those seasons. I try to express them without being assured of their validity. This is especially true when it comes to God. I simply have to trust and believe that God is there. Even when—and especially when—I can't feel God.

But sometimes I want to feel God. I *need* to feel God. I need to feel deep down in my bones that God is still here and that God loves me. In depressions, I can't even tell you what that feeling feels like. I'm so far from it. Does it feel like a warm tingling? Like tears during a moving gospel song? Like the warm biscuits my Nana made while singing "Jesus Keep Me Near the Cross" as she ambled around the kitchen? Does it feel like the wood at the altar of St. Paul AME Church in Cambridge, where I once knew God so powerfully? I don't remember. I don't know. I can't get to it.

My desire to feel God does not even invoke it. Wanting to feel God does not lead to me actually feeling God. Desire is simply desire. My want is only met with greater emptiness.

It becomes tiring: to write and teach and preach about God without feeling God. To pray and sing and worship without feeling God. While depression probably makes this more acute for me (since I can't feel anything good in these times), I understand that this is also part of the spiritual life. There will be winters when the only evidence of life is deep below ground. (Renita Weems writes beautifully about this in her book *Listening for God*.)

And maybe this is what I like so much about Holy Week. This is where we see Jesus' most desperate humanity. This is where we see Jesus thirst and feel forsaken. We also see Jesus surrender.

It amazes me that Jesus can continue to minister while in such pain and emptiness. It amazes me when I can.

∾

Exploration
What do you do when you can't feel God?

Reflection
What can you actually do even when you don't feel God?

impatience

I'm not a big fan of self-help books. It's not that they don't contain any wisdom or truth. It's just that I prefer—perhaps even need—more human interaction. But let's be honest, a book is far cheaper than a life coach, therapist, or weekly lunch with a good friend. And self-help books remind us that we ourselves play a significant role in finding the answers to many of our challenges. The books often do this through a combination of straight-talk, tough love, and encouragement.

Like this one: "Life is difficult."

These are the opening words to M. Scott Peck's famous book *The Road Less Traveled*. Originally published in 1978, *The Road Less Traveled* continues to be a self-help classic.

In this opening line, Peck tells a simple truth that no one with a depressive condition forgets. Even people who don't live with a depressive condition know that life is difficult. But, Peck says, many people spend a lot of energy complaining about, denying, or avoiding the fact that life is difficult. Once we accept this axiom, life is no longer difficult.

Peck offers several approaches to managing the complexities of life. His discussion of "delayed gratification" has always grabbed my attention. Most people call this concept "sacrificing present comfort for future gain." Peck describes it as a "process of scheduling the pain and pleasure of life in such a way as to enhance the pleasure by meeting and experiencing the pain first and getting it over with." My faith tradition calls it *patience*.

It may well be a deep spiritual wisdom: there is merit in waiting.

The psalmist writes it this way: "Weeping may endure for a night, but joy comes in the morning" (30:5).

The prophet Isaiah puts it this way: "They that wait on God will renew their strength; they will mount up with wings like eagles; they will run and not get weary; they will walk and not faint" (40:31).

People who live with a depressive condition know a lot about delayed gratification. We're constantly waiting—waiting for the medicine to kick in, waiting for the fog to lift, waiting for the pain to subside, waiting to feel better enough to do regular activities, waiting to feel again.

This kind of waiting is a characteristic of the public life I have chosen as well. There's a good deal of delayed gratification in being a scholar and an activist. There's a lot of education that must happen before earning an advanced degree and an academic job. There's a lot of on-the-ground work, reaching out, phone calls, and poorly attended meetings before sensing that a difference has been made.

I know how to wait. I understand how to delay gratification. I—and many other people—do it all the time.

But that doesn't mean I like it.

There is a significant part of me that wants what I want when I want it. And as M. Scott Peck reminds us, delayed gratification involves pain. Platitudes about enjoying the process or finding joy in the journey don't help. And biblical verses about the value of waiting don't actually make it any easier for me.

My internal brat speaks another maxim: waiting sucks!

With so much of my life in delayed gratification mode, I realize that I sometimes need to foster my own impatience. I need some kind of immediate gratification. I actually *need* to see the fruits of my efforts in a relatively short period of time. Sometimes I need to know I'm making a difference so I can continue on with the hard work. Sometimes I need a deep hearty laugh until the big breakthrough.

So I schedule it. I actually plan activities where there's little waiting for the payoff. I take up all kinds of hobbies that allow me to see beauty quickly.

- I make jewelry for myself.
- I cook.
- I rent a funny stand-up-comedy video.

In less than two hours, I have received some kind of pay-off. Something to hold me while I'm waiting.

Down deep, I think M. Scott Peck is right. Delayed gratification is a good thing. It helps foster love, discipline, success, and spiritual depth. But it's not easy, especially when waiting to feel human and alive again.

In the meanwhile, I think it's okay to nurture the impatience a little. It makes the waiting bearable.

≈

Exploration
What do you do when you are waiting?

Reflection
What things can give you immediate gratification?

quiet crash

In *Their Eyes Were Watching God*, Zora Neale Hurston writes about the protagonist Janie Crawford's relationships with her three husbands, and how they reveal her evolving relationship with herself. During an argument with her second husband, Janie realizes that "something fell off the shelf inside of her." That wasn't the end of the relationship, but it was, in hindsight, when she knew it was over.

I've often used this phrase when talking with my friends about the breaking up of interpersonal relationships. There are, I opine from my own experience, three breakups. There's the moment when you really break up, yeah, but there are two other ones. On the tail end of a break up, there's that time when you're finally over the person. When you stop crying, stop missing, stop pining, stop being angry, and stop substituting your former lover with new lovers. That's the final breakup.

But there's an initial breakup: the breakup before the breakup. There's the moment when something falls off the shelf inside of you. It's the moment when deep inside yourself, you know it's over. It can be months or years between this moment and the actual breakup, but it did happen. It's quiet. It's almost imperceptible. You kind of know it when it happens, but you usually only really know it in hindsight. It's when something has been said or done or expressed—something has happened. And you realize that there's no turning back. This is it. Something broke. Something fell off the shelf. Something died.

The death of depression is a lot like that. It's quiet. It's invisible. It's not like a rotting egg or broken vase. There are no sensory signs. There's no audible crash. Some time when you weren't paying attention. Some time while you were trying desperately to get up, get dressed, and go to work. Some time when you gave all your energy to making dinner for the children. Some time while you were trying to eke life out of lifelessness . . . something died. And because there was no unbearable stench, or spine-curdling scream, or shards of glass on the floor, you missed it.

Because your breath never stopped, you thought you were still alive.

And so the death of depression, like that first breakup, may not reveal itself for awhile. It took me three years to realize that I died in depression. It was three long years from the incident that sent me in a downward spiral and the moment I realized that something died that night. I spent most of those three years trying to put one foot in front of the other. Trying to protect my relationships and my career from my internal desperation. I spent a lot of those years angry about what had happened. My journal is filled with various phrasings of these words: "I WANT MY LIFE BACK!" I spent most of those years trying to get my predepression life back.

It took me three years—and a lot of therapy—to stop fighting. I had to stop fighting the fact that I wasn't going to get back what I lost. I could not unring the bell. I could not go back in time. My experiences had changed me. I could remember who I was, but I could not go back to being that woman.

The words from the ancient Greek philosopher Heraclitus were truer than I could have imagined when I learned them in college: "No man ever steps in the same river twice, for it's not the same river and he's not the same man."

It's poetic. It's also a hard, ugly truth: When you come back from the dead, you aren't the same person.

Although I'm still unsure about whether or not Jesus was physically transported vertically into the clouds like in those old Renaissance paintings, I understand why he could not stay long after the resurrection. He could not return to his old life. He could not continue to walk and teach and heal the way he did before the crucifixion. Surely this is what the disciples expected. They expected him to be back, for good, and to the tenth power. It's only human to expect that.

I suspect that Jesus knew that wasn't possible. It was not the same river. He was not the same man.

I wonder why we ask something of ourselves that Jesus did not ask of himself. I wonder why we experience monumental losses and deaths and try to pretend like nothing has changed. We go to work. We go to our faith communities. We go to meetings. We keep the same schedule. We wash our faces and trim our hair so we don't even look different.

Why do we hide our own deaths in ways we would never hide the physical death of a loved one? Don't we love ourselves?

When Jesus died on the cross, the disciples gathered to mourn and cry. When the risen Jesus left, the disciples gathered to pray and worship. I think those are appropriate responses to loss. After all, this is what my family does when someone dies. We cry. And then we sing their favorite songs, laugh about the funny things they did, and pray for one another.

There are moments when I wish I had known sooner. I wish I had heard the crashing of that thing inside of me. I wish I had not wasted time trying to get back to something I could never reach. I wish I had recognized the death when it happened. That's nearly impossible, though. Because I wanted to live, I had to give all my attention to that. I lacked the ability to reflect on what was dying. I was unable to be philosophical or pedagogical or wise. *To be any of those things* required stability.

In the three years it took me to realize I had died, I became someone new. Someone I actually liked. Someone who could not have been born had I not died. Once I knew that, everything else became easier. I could mourn and live again.

Now I just wish for community. I wish that other people could see me dying—even when I can't see it for myself. Even before I know *what* has died. In these quiet deaths, I'd like to have others who will mourn and cry and worship and pray with me.

For how long? Until.

Until I'm stable. Until I can acknowledge the death for myself. Until it's not so hard to eat and sleep and work. Until I accept and welcome the person I've become in the new life. Until—as Jesus says in his ascension speech to the disciples (Luke 24:49)—until the power comes.

∾

Exploration
When has something crashed off the shelf inside of you?
What was broken?

Reflection
Who are you becoming since the crash?

empty

My favorite slogan of the environmental movement is the edict that we should:

Live simply so others can simply live.

It's a basic truism that most of us who are living in the world's wealthiest nations find incredibly difficult to enact. The everyday components of our lives—driving to work, flying to visit family and friends, buying a plastic bottle of water, printing out important documents, using our cell phones—contribute to the planet's disease and the diminishment in the life quality of our brothers and sisters in the poorest nations. Even the most ecologically conscious of us have a difficult time living in this country without contributing to global environmental problems. We cannot escape participating in a system so dependent on excess.

Yet this slogan aims to remind us that we don't need to have it all. We can be content with enough. We need enough food to stave off hunger and provide nutrition, enough shelter to keep us safe and warm.

I believe that this is what monks and nuns mean when they take vows of poverty. They are not poor. Rather they embrace lives of simplicity: a room, a desk, a chair, a lamp, a bed, warm bread, spiritual community.

This kind of living is the opposite of the religious messages that talk about abundance and prosperity. The Jewish and Christian traditions have scriptures that speak of having blessings so great that God will "throw open the floodgates of heaven and pour out so much blessing that you will not have room enough for it" (Malachi 3:10) or that we will receive gifts in such quantity that they will be "pressed down, shaken together, running over" (Luke 6:38).

Other scriptures suggest that plenty is the reward for faithfulness:

- "Therefore keep the words of this covenant, and do them, that you may prosper in all that you do," (Deuteronomy 29:9).
- "The plans of the diligent lead surely to plenty, but those of everyone who is hasty, surely to poverty" (Proverbs 21:5).
- Even Jesus indicates that he came so that we can "have life and life more abundantly" (John 10:10).

These seem to be the opposite of the simple life for which our planet and economy are calling.

So I want to say that the times have changed. Perhaps we should not apply the lessons of ancient communities that occupied no more land than the state of Maine to contemporary global society. But, on the other hand, should we forget those lessons?

Even in those ancient times, expectations for plenty were balanced with periodic and ritual emptying. If the harvest was plenty, the temple sacrifice was large. Crops were to be left in the fields for the poor to glean for their own food. Debts and oppressions were released every seven years during the season of Jubilee. Even the early followers of Jesus came together and shared their belongings as they focused on worship and the sharing of their faith. Receiving came after, and as a result of, giving.

This leads me to believe that there is a principle we have missed in the emphasis on abundance and plenty:

Fullness is balanced by emptiness.

This is a difficult concept for me as someone who lives with a depressive condition. For the most part, "emptiness" is a bad thing.

- "Emptiness" is the word I use to describe how vacuous and lonely my soul can feel, even in the presence of people who say they love me.
- "Emptiness" is the word I use to describe the challenge of having to teach, write, and work when the only nourishment I have is the toast and peanut butter I made myself eat—despite my loss of appetite.
- "Emptiness" is the word I use to describe the groping for something to steady my wavering sense of self until I can find my way on the path again—assuming that I still believe that there is a path.
- Emptiness is hunger, thirst, and the hollow sound of nothingness against the tin metal of my soul.

No matter how you slice it, "emptiness" is not something I desire.

"Fullness" is what I revel in and cling to when it's around, because I know fullness will not last forever. It will subside again. Into deep, dark emptiness.

For this reason, I've always felt a disconnection when I hear sermons and lessons about how Christ emptied self in the process of incarnation.

> Let the same mind be in you that was in Christ Jesus,
> who, though he was in the form of God, did not re-
> gard equality with God as something to be exploited,
> but *emptied himself*, taking the form of a slave, being
> born in human likeness. And being found in human
> form, he humbled himself and became obedient to the
> point of death—even death on a cross. (Philippians
> 2:5-8)

Christian traditions have interpreted this passage in a variety of ways. Some say that God relinquishes divine attributes of omnipotence, holiness, perfection, and so forth, while present in the historical figure of Jesus. That's how Jesus is fully human and fully divine. Others say that Jesus intentionally hid his true divinity and glory by coming to the common people in a humble manner. Still others will say that God constantly pours out Godself in the beauty and wonder of creation.

Despite these theological trajectories, Paul's message seems clear:

- Imitate Jesus' self-emptying and be subservient to others.
- Sacrifice.
- Empty yourself in order to receive God—in order to be like God.

Given my experiences of emptiness, this does not feel holy to me. It does not feel like God. Surely God wouldn't consider any kind of emptiness as an ideal, as something I should emulate.

I am left with questions: Can't God fill us without displacing us? Without needing us to become empty vessels? Without asking us to lose whatever sense of being we have finally found?

Every part of me tells me to reject this understanding of who Jesus is and how we should understand salvation. When the preachers and teachers speak of *kenosis* (the Greek word for "emptying"), I close my ears. "Not my God," I think.

Recently, I've begun to reconsider.

I decided to throw a party for twenty of my closest friends. I cleaned my home thoroughly. I pushed some furniture and books to the walls and closets. I pulled out folding chairs and stools, imagining where I would fit so many people into the corners of the living and dining rooms. I bought pounds of beans, bunches of vegetables, bags of rice and meal. I began cooking two days early. The first guest arrived at 6:30 AM; the last guest did not leave until 10 PM. By the end of the day, I had cooked, fed, laughed, danced, hugged, listened to, and chatted with people I don't see nearly enough. And I fell onto the bed fully clothed, bone-tired. Empty.

I felt how my full house and full kitchen had made me empty. And this emptiness left me feeling full of love, friendship, and purpose.

Is this the lesson of emptiness and fullness? That we should share what we have? Could this be why Jesus tells so many parables about how a host has a celebration, banquet, and feast, and we are all invited?

Perhaps hospitality is my window into understanding that living simply, experiencing God in our bodies, and being like our spiritual models begin with the childhood lesson to share.

This could be just as true for global politics and the unequal distribution of wealth as it is for my small apartment and circle of friends.

And when we can't get there, because we're running on empty, may someone open her doors, cook a meal, pull the chair back from the table, and share with us.

∾

Exploration
What makes you feel empty?

Reflection
When do you feel full?

lost and found

A couple of weeks ago, I reached in my wallet and could not find my credit card. I had not used it in hours and could not put my hand on it after searching my bag and couch. I started looking for the phone number of the last place where I had purchased something. I was fairly calm because I knew it had not yet been stolen and misused. I knew this because my credit card comes with great fraud protection. Whenever a charge appears that is slightly different from my normal purchases, I receive a phone call from my credit card company. This verification call notes that something is unusual, and they want to verify that I'm okay and that I'm in possession of my card.

It's a wonderfully personalized lost and found system. In my experience, looking for something that is lost is much more like rummaging. Like the time when my friend's child lost his second winter hat in one season and swore he didn't know where it was. My friend and I went to the elementary school and found a box of lost and found items waist high to an adult. We turned over the box and dug through misplaced child-sized coats, mittens, toys, lunch boxes, and scarves. In that pile were both hats—and the mittens we didn't even know the child had lost. After twenty or thirty minutes, we came out of the box feeling victorious!

Finding something that was lost gives us feelings of both relief and joy.

Jesus refers to that joy when he tells the story of the lost coin. The parable of the lost coin is sandwiched between the well-known story of the prodigal son who returns home and the story of the shepherd who leaves the ninety-nine sheep to go find the one that is lost.

In this parable, a woman has ten coins, and then she loses one. She turns on all the lights and sweeps under everything, looking for the one coin she has lost.

At first read, this story pales in comparison to the story of the sheep and the father and his sons. Then I thought about it in a different way.

There are times when I have counted out exact change for something: going to the Laundromat or getting on the bus or putting coins in the parking meter. It's usually not a lot of money, but it is the money needed for a certain task. If I lose a quarter, I go searching for it. It's only 25 cents, but I need that coin to do what I need to do.

I imagine this woman throwing cushions off the couch, lifting up the bed covers, picking things up off the table, getting on her hands and knees, ignoring the dust that accumulates under furniture. Searching. Rummaging. Until she finds the coin.

When she finds it, she calls her friends and neighbors to rejoice over having found the quarter. That, Jesus tells us, is how the company of heaven rejoices when we draw closer to God.

These images of people searching for missing items matter to me when I experience depression as a state of being lost. There are times when that seems the best way to talk about what it's like to be depressed.

- I am tangled inside my mind's endless thoughts of how inadequate I am.

- I become a stranger to myself—feeling and acting in ways that don't seem like me.
- I can't imagine feeling happy again.
- I am adrift among the various demands of my life: I acknowledge them, but I can't feel anything.
- I can't find my way to the vibrant world that's outside a seemingly impenetrable window.
- I believe that no one can see who I really am or how I feel, and even if they could, I'm not worth their time, their effort, or their concern.

I feel lost.

I fantasize about a world where my friends and colleagues are like the fraud protection of my credit card company. They would know my typical patterns of behavior. They could see that these reveal my values and priorities. They would notice if things were unusual and say, "She is not acting like herself." They would check in with me to see if I were okay. They would ask security questions to make sure that I am the person they know I long to be, the person I need to be.

Loving and caring for someone with a depressive condition is probably like looking for the lost hat or lost coin. It involves sifting through a lot of mundane and unpleasant stuff. It's not so obvious if a person is having a bad day, another medical challenge, or is slipping away into a depressive state. It requires taking time out of one's day or maybe even stopping everything one is doing. They would do it because they want their loved one to feel warm and cozy in the world. They do it because they need their loved one in their life.

Many wonderful organizations, books, and programs can help people to identify "lost" behavior in loved ones. They offer various techniques for searching for someone. They offer support while one is sifting through the dust bunnies and clothing piles to try to find a friend or loved one.

I have some people in my life who can hear that I am lost from the sound of my voice. Others seem to be oblivious. I take great comfort in the belief that even when my closest friends do not do all of this to find me, God does.

I usually turn to God first when I feel lost. It's a kind of reversal. When I am lost, I behave as though I must find myself. I search for the place where I am supposed to be. I yearn for a roadmap back home.

When I am lost, I go to church to get found. While I trust that God is everywhere—even nearer than my closest breath—something miraculous happens for me at church. There are hugs around my legs from children, a liturgy I know by heart, and music I can clap or dance to. There's something miraculous in kneeling at a wooden altar or hearing a message about God's unconditional love.

Unless or until my friends and family come looking for me, the combination of these things makes me feel found. They make me feel that I am safely back in the palm of God's hand.

~

Exploration
What do you do when you feel lost?

Reflection
How do you get found again?

unbreakable

In M. Night Shyamalan's 2000 movie *Unbreakable*, two characters are juxtaposed: Elijah Price (played by Samuel L. Jackson) and David Dunn (played by Bruce Willis). Elijah Price was born with Type I osteogenesis imperfecta (also known as "Brittle Bone Disease"); his body does not make the kind of collagen that strengthens his bones. Thus, his bones break easily. In fact, he was born with broken limbs. On the other hand, David Dunn has extraordinary strength and lives through accidents and catastrophes that kill most people. He comes out of them without even a scratch. He seems to be unbreakable.

Elijah tracks down David, and presents him with a theory that suggests that they are the remnants of an ancient system of storytelling where superheroes and their archenemies are based on real people like themselves: each other's exact opposite.

While this movie has all the drama of a psychological thriller and the power of comic book and legendary storytelling, it's an oddly familiar assumption. Many aspects of our culture function as if there are "unbreakable" people in our midst.

I often hear it in variations of the quote by the nineteenth-century philosopher Friedrich Nietzsche:

That which does not kill us makes us stronger.

Paul says the same thing very lyrically in 2 Corinthians 4:8-9:

> We are hard-pressed on every side, yet not crushed;
> we are perplexed, but not in despair; persecuted, but
> not forsaken; struck down, but not destroyed.

While I won't deny the personal experiences of Nietzsche or Paul, as general platitudes I think there are few more damaging lies.

In the face of ideas like these, many people believe that they should act like comic book superheroes. They believe that when they endure terrible emotional and physical events, they should emerge triumphantly. They *should* be a wiser, stronger, and shinier version of who they were before. Some theologies (like the theory of redemptive suffering in its purest form) state that it is only through suffering that individuals and communities can achieve salvation or positive transformation.

And so many people suppress how painful some elements of their lives really are because they are busy trying to show that they have it together. They are trying to show that they are unbreakable.

I acknowledge that many of us have to keep moving forward in the face of illness and trauma and danger because our families and households are physically and financially dependent on our ability to go to work and make an income. Nevertheless, I fault societal structures for their inability to recognize and support people who are crumbling inside.

So I'll say it again: this idea that what doesn't kill us serves to make us stronger is one of life's more damaging lies. If only because life experience will teach us that there *are* things that kill us. And for those who do not die, some do not come out stronger or more encouraged. Some people come out of life's traumas and sufferings as weaker, demoralized, and emptier shells of who they were.

The fact that some people can survive difficulty, pain, death, sickness, and war is somehow attached to the grace and power of God. But the difference between those of us who survive and those of us who do not should not be measured by our level of faith, prayer, devotion, or inner fortitude. It's better measured by access to informed and attentive friends, loving communities, healing resources, and societal acceptance.

As someone who lives with a depressive condition, I'm aware of how quickly I can become like the character of Elijah Price. Every small thing will cause me to question myself, my friends, and my abilities. When I'm struggling to do the most basic tasks of daily living, I feel weak. I feel like a shell of a human being. It doesn't take much for me to feel broken inside.

Perhaps like Elijah, we will seek out or even yearn for that which is unbreakable. I know I do. I want to return to the part of myself that can survive great odds and come out stronger and wiser. I want to live up to the ideal that I ought to be able to manage difficulty with more grace, finesse, and gratitude. "Why," I ask myself, "don't I feel perplexed without feeling despair? Why don't I feel persecution without feeling forsaken? Why aren't I more ... unbreakable?"

The movie again serves as inspiration. As David Dunn explores his past, he realizes that he has a weakness—a weakness that can kill him. (I won't give it away, in case you want to rent the movie.) Elijah, a comic book aficionado, reminds the viewer that all superheroes have these weaknesses. This acknowledgment means more than just saying that we all have our personal Achilles' heel, kryptonite, or, as Paul says, thorns in our flesh (2 Corinthians 12:7). Rather, I hear this as another statement of truth:

No one is unbreakable. Not even superheroes.

This is an especially important maxim for those of us who live with depressive or disabling conditions. When we imagine that there is an ideal of perfection and strength to which we do not attain, we need to remember again: no one is unbreakable.

As a black woman, I find this idea and its debunking always in my orbit. In the late 1970s, the black feminist Michele Wallace wrote *Black Macho and the Myth of the Superwoman.* More recently, the Crunk Feminist Collective blogged about black women and depression and declared, "Life is not a fairytale." My colleague Chanequa Walker-Barnes at Shaw University Divinity School does excellent work on the religious and psychological damage of the idea of a "strong black woman."

I don't think this is at all particular to black women. I think this ideal of being unbreakable is something we all need to resist. We need to resist this because there are messages in society and religion that reinforce this idea. We need to resist this because life experience shows us it's not true. We need to resist this so we can offer ourselves greater grace.

~

Exploration
How have you tried to seem unbreakable?

Reflection
How can you resist the myth of being unbreakable?

silence

I've long felt that the Christmas season begins too early and ends too soon. This is not a religious complaint. It's a commercial complaint. In the consumer culture of the United States, Christmas decorations appear in drugstores and grocery markets before Halloween. By mid-October, I feel inundated with red and green paper, images of Santa Claus, and ringing bells. By late November, evergreen trees can be found for sale in parking lots, and retailers are announcing sales. Whether one is walking down the street, watching television, or caroling door-to-door with other people, the sounds of Christmas can be heard for nearly two months.

And then, on December 26, it's all over. The day after Christmas yields even bigger sales at retailers, and the discarded trees begin to line the gutters of neighborhoods. The celebrated joy and hope and gifts of the season end abruptly. The cacophony of Christmas skids to a halting silence.

It is in this silence that I want more Christmas. In the weeks after the jubilee has ended, I'm still pondering the biblical scriptures that discuss the circumstances of Jesus' birth. No matter how our crèches and nativity scenes are arranged, I know it is in the days, weeks, and months *after* Jesus' birth that the shepherds and magi arrive. In these days and weeks, the baby Jesus cries, and Joseph and Mary rock, soothe, lose sleep, and offer sustenance as new parents have for centuries. In this time, a baby's small face takes shape to look like the parents or grandparents; a tiny personality begins to emerge; the eyes open and search for the image attached to the familiar voices.

I have this feeling that just when society gets quiet and bored . . . just when the big celebration is over . . . in the silence of our memories . . . life becomes more nuanced, and growth actually begins.

I suspect that Mary was aware of this and honored it. As the Gospel of Luke recounts the narrative of Jesus' birth, there are shepherds and declarations and rejoicing. Holding her newborn in her arms, Mary "kept all these things and pondered them in her heart" (Luke 2:19).

I hear Mary's own silence amid the activity around her.

As someone who lives with a depressive condition, I find it to be an apt description for how my depressions must appear to those around me.

Silence.

When the days become shorter and the darkness of the night lingers well past the time of waking and beginning work, I become quieter. My heart becomes heavy with the grief of missing a parent and grandparents during holy days. My mind is cloudy, and I'm lucky to have two or three clear intellectual thoughts in a day. My feelings are described in monotone syllables: bad, sad, blue, gray, ugh. My ability to multitask wanes. I lose hours doing pretty much nothing while the dishes piles up, the work accumulates, and I don't even care.

I slow down. I interact with fewer people. I go dark. I am silent.

This is how I feel to myself. So I imagine that from the outside, where there was once activity and vigor, there is now merely silence. No matter the energy and vigor of a holiday season, I feel that I have retreated. And, unlike the abrupt ending of the commercial season of Christmas, I cannot turn myself on and off like a switch, discarding my blues on the curb of my public life.

I cling to Mary's model of silence in the midst of the celebration and chaos around her. I take everything in, but my responses are rather sedate. I focus on small details that can sustain me. When Mary must have reveled in the days and weeks of a baby reaching to hold a finger, the gradual formation of nasal tissue, the constant rocking and cooing, I too focus on small details: I laughed today; a friend came by and made me leave the house; a certain color sweater makes my eyes look brighter.

This is what depression in the midst of celebration looks like for me. Externally, I power down. Internally, I churn everything over and over inside of myself, looking for whatever will get me from one day to the next. And all of this is a very quiet process.

From my conversations with other people who live with depression conditions, I feel rather secure in saying that I'm not the only one.

This is why I want more Christmas. I want the Christmas season to continue in the silence after the end of the sales, so we can remember that Mary and Joseph experienced a similar silence. I want to pay attention to Mary's life after Jesus' birth. I want someone to honor the silences of those carried in the currents of work and faith community activities.

This is harder. It's hard to hear silences.

Mental health challenges don't often come to the forefront of society's attention until they explode or are otherwise noisy. Suicides, shootings, and shouting are more apt to bring to mind those who live with these challenges than anything else. And yet when we stop to ponder even these tormented lives, the reports come out: she or he was often alone or never said much or never fought back.

Silence.

So maybe I want these silences to be more than just honored. I want the silences to become a signal of internal churning. I want people to notice who's not there and who's not talking and who's not writing and who's not celebrating—the silent. Perhaps the silent are just taking it all in. Pondering.

But perhaps the silent have powered down, gone dark, and need someone to shine a light of presence for the days and weeks and months until the next season of life begins again.

~

Exploration
What is happening inside when you are silent to those around you?

Reflection
What small details can sustain you in the midst of silence?

well enough

Like most people I know, I have a very long to-do list. It seems that I add things faster than I cross them off. I use the list for my much-needed sense of accomplishment. I exact this need in all types of ways. For example, I refuse to let the servers in restaurants refill my water glass until I've nearly finished it. That constant refilling makes me feel as if I've never finished drinking my water; it takes my sense of accomplishment away. When it comes to my to-do list, I'll often add basic things to it just so I can cross them off. Things like: wake up, get dressed, eat breakfast, wash dishes, drive to work. On most days, that means five things have been crossed off my list before I get to the real work.

Of course there are days when I hate the to-do list. It seems to go on forever and have a personal spiteful disposition that says, "You will never get it all done." But the to-do list itself is not evil. It's there to help jog my memory, organize my activities, and establish priorities.

Truth be told, the to-do list gets long and weighty when I make decisions in my I-can-conquer-the-world-in-one-day mindset. I don't feel superhuman, but I do feel smart and very capable. Yes, I can write that article, review that essay, speak at that conference, sit on those committees, host those functions, start a study group, read four new books, finish writing my own books, fly cross-country three weekends a month . . . you get the idea.

When I feel well, I really can do all this. And I can do it with a pretty high level of quality.

When I don't feel well, I use up all my energy on those first five items:

- Wake up.
- Get dressed.
- Eat breakfast.
- Wash dishes.
- Drive to work.

In fact, this is how I measure my depressive condition: by how hard or easy it is to do the basic things.

This has been the best gauge of my depressions. Depression doesn't hit me like the drop from walking off of a cliff. It's slow, subtle, and downright sneaky. The things on the list that once seemed doable become monkeys on my back. I want to shake them off so I can focus on the top five.

I organize my life into lists. Sometimes this is very helpful. Like the time a certain airline lost my luggage. At home, I had a list of every item that was in the suitcase because I made the list when I packed. I also had a corresponding receipt. I was fully reimbursed.

I've also made lists in my faith life. In a season when I focused intensely on my spiritual growth, I made a list of the things I should be doing every day:

- Pray for friends.
- Pray for family members.
- Pray for people I don't like.

- Pray for myself.
- Pray for the world.
- Read and reflect on a biblical passage.
- Prepare for teaching weekly Bible study.
- Talk with at least one of my Bible study members.
- Communicate with my spiritual leader.
- Make arrangements for getting to church.
- Brainstorm ideas for young adult group activities at church.

The list continued. I scheduled the list's activities in a chart with appropriate time allotments so that I could fit them in with my other commitments. While these are all good things, I continually set myself up for failure. It's a fairly unsustainable list for someone who isn't a nun, monk, or full-time minister—and then it's still asking a lot.

While I can acknowledge that this was my overachiever, type-A personality dipped in religion, it was also a product of my faith life. I loved God and wanted to develop a relationship with God. I believed that all these things would facilitate intimacy with God. I was taught that intimacy with God was similar to intimacy with people: it required time and investment. I wanted God to be happy with me. I believed that doing certain things would please God, just as doing certain things would displease God. I didn't want to displease God. I didn't want to commit the sins against which I heard preachers and Sunday school teachers and Christian leaders admonish. I wanted to do God's will. I wanted to be blessed and favored. The list helped me get there.

It would take years for me to realize that God does not want me to have a legalistic faith. God will not disown me, walk out on me, or lose my number if I don't pray every day. God is not waiting to shake a finger of shame at me if I do something that indicates I am human. God just wants me. That's enough.

Jesus kept trying to tell his disciples the same thing. He used a metaphor that his agrarian audience would understand: a mustard seed.

- "The kingdom of God is like a mustard seed . . ." It's small, but it will grow into a large bush (Matthew 13:31-32; Mark 4:30-32; Luke 13:18-20).
- "If you have faith the size of a mustard seed, the mountain would move . . ." (Matthew 17:19-21).
- "If you have faith the size of a mustard seed, you could say to this tree, move . . ." (Luke 17:5-7).

I've seen a mustard seed (I use it when I make curry spices). It's small. This isn't to say that we only need a little faith to perform miracles—and you don't even have that much! (That's the message I've heard in sermons.) Rather, I understand Jesus to be saying:

You already have enough.

I need this kind of message as I make it through my to-do lists. Whether the list is completed or not, I try to tell myself, "You've already done enough."

Most of my life is not lived on the depressed end of the top-five items or on the far end, where I can actually do everything on the list in one day and exercise, get eight hours of sleep, and be a good parent, lover, friend, daughter, minister, and professor. I don't bounce from one end to the other. Most of my life is spent somewhere in the middle.

Jesus is right. It doesn't take a whole lot to be enough. Even if all I can do is the top five, I am well enough.

My friend Andre Myers, a composer, wrote a song for children living with cancer. The refrain perfectly captures the attitude I try

to have most days—whether I'm moving mountains or tapped out
by list item number six:

> *Because I'm well enough to hear the goodness*
> *in a loving song*
> *and I am well enough to feel night's beauty*
> *dance into the dawn*
> *and I am well enough to love the person*
> *that I strive to be*
> *and I'm just well enough to know that I am strong*
> *just being me*

～

Exploration
What five things are enough for you on any given day?

Reflection
How do you know when you are well enough?

sin?

I like to do crossword puzzles in free moments. I was in trouble when I discovered the iPod/iPhone app. I wish I could say I do them because of the new research that indicates that mental games like crosswords and Sudoku stave off Alzheimer's disease. I'm not that forward-looking. I find that games with repetition and moderate levels of mental attention help to manage anxiety. Yes, I'm claiming health care in solitaire, word search, and crossword puzzles.

There's a consistent crossword question and answer that catches my attention as a religious professional. In various ways the clue reads, "topic of sermons." The answer is always "sin."

I find it slightly problematic that some element of popular culture assumes that all sermons are about sin. After all, preachers talk about grace, love, justice, forgiveness, prayer, and hope—to name a few. But I guess there's some truth in the fact that "sin" is the special purview of religious folk. I say something like this when I tell my students that questions about evil are philosophical and "sin" is a theological category. Sin isn't just about what's wrong in the world. Sin is things that God doesn't like.

As a theologian who teaches in an ecumenical and increasingly multifaith institution, I teach a variety of theological perspectives. I give my students a longer version of this speech:

Theology is how we think about God. There are lots of ways to think about God. We can see from the history of Christianity that there have always been many ways to think about God. God is bigger than all of the ways we approach God. Our theologies are affected by our experiences, traditions, and interpretations of scripture and by how it makes sense when we put it together (we call this the Wesleyan quadrilateral). I'm less interested in what you believe than in how you believe. That is, I'm hoping to teach you about how to think theologically, systematically (if that's the class), and in historical and contemporary contexts.

For this reason, I teach evangelical, process, liberation, classical, Protestant, and Catholic theologies together.

I've tried to take this approach when looking at the category of sin. The German feminist theologian Dorothee Sölle summarizes three major approaches in her book *Thinking About God*. While these are somewhat reductionist, I think the typology is helpful: Orthodox perspectives think of sin as disobedience. Liberal perspectives consider estrangement from God as sin. Liberation theologies think about oppression in the world as sin.

They all agree that when we sin, we don't just hurt each other. We also hurt God.

This connects to depressive conditions because there is an all-too-common assertion that committing suicide is a sin. In fact, it is an unforgivable sin. In *Lay My Burden Down: Suicide and the Mental Health Crisis Among African Americans*, Dr. Alvin Poussaint and Amy Alexander assert that this religious teaching contributes to many people's silence about suicidal ideation. Because people are afraid of the religious consequences of contemplating suicide, they often do not seek help—which can contribute to their mental health challenge.

I've tried to apply my theological reasoning to the notion that suicide is an unforgivable sin. From what I understand, the logic goes this way: When a person is born and when a person dies are part of God's sovereign plan and will. When a person takes her own life, she is violating this sovereignty of God. Because suicide is willfully done against the spirit of God's life in us, it blasphemes the Holy Spirit—and this is what Jesus said was an unforgivable sin. Suicide is unforgivable because, unlike in the case of murder, for example, the person never has the opportunity to repent and be forgiven by God. Suicide is also an indication that a person cannot handle what is happening in his life even though part of the Bible indicates that God will not give anyone more than he can bear. After all, scripture indicates that God gives us love, power, self-control; hundreds of persecuted folk in history have leaned on God's power to make it through difficult times.

I understand that this understanding of sin falls under the larger rubric of considering sin as disobedience to God, God's laws, and God's will. While there are other Christian theological approaches to sin (like the ones I mentioned above), this is a common one. It is connected to a wider understanding of how one believes God relates to the world. What kind of power does God have? Does God know what we are going to do before we are going to do it? Can God stop certain things from happening while permitting others? If so, how does God decide which ones? What is the role of human agency? These are the kinds of questions theologians seek to answer. They become especially real in the face of suicide.

Everything in me resists the idea that suicide is a sin. I say this because I've been suicidal and I love many other people who have been suicidal. When a person is suicidal, she is not thinking about going against God's will.

- She's thinking that she'll never feel better again.
- She's thinking that the pain is so intense that only death can alleviate it.
- She's thinking that her care is a burden on everyone she loves.
- She's thinking that she's incapable of making a positive contribution to the world.
- She's thinking that the world, including her loved ones, will be better off without her.
- She's thinking that God hates her for making her this sad, morose, numb, and/or bad.
- She's thinking that she has tried every medication, every therapist, every insurance agency, everything—and none of it has helped.
- She's thinking that she has exhausted the love and patience of her family and friends.
- She's thinking that there is no way to escape how horrible she feels.

Broadly speaking, this is what it's like for people who are suicidal, many of whom are young people. Are you aware of the following?

- Suicide is the third leading cause of death for fifteen- to twenty-four-year-olds.
- Suicide is the second leading cause of death for twenty-five- to thirty-four-year-olds.
- Suicide is the second leading cause of death among college students.
- There are four male deaths by suicide for each female death by suicide.
- More people die from suicide than from homicide.
- About eleven attempted suicides occur for every suicide death.

- Lesbian, gay, bisexual, transgender, and questioning youth are up to four times more likely to attempt suicide than their heterosexual peers.

Did all these people sin? Did they do something unforgivable? Should we believe they're in hell, even if a rationally consistent theological argument can be made for that belief?

There's one other thing I share with my theology students: we all have "norms." That is, we all have normative markers by which we must measure theological claims. It's the things that tell us something is wrong and something else is right. Many people use the Golden Rule as a norm. If so, they would ask themselves, "Does this theology support or violate treating others the way I want to be treated?" Others like the Love principles. They would ask, "Does this support or violate the assertion that God is love and that we are to love one another?"

One of my norms centers around God's omnipresence. I ask:

Does this idea support or violate this core principle of my faith?
God is with us.

Supporting the idea that suicide is an unforgivable sin suggests that God has abandoned someone in his deepest time of need. It suggests that God is more interested in laws and providence than people's souls. It suggests that God could end pain but allows it in the interest of a philosophical principle. Everything I know about God seems to indicate that God doesn't do that.

If there is any commonality between sin and suicide, it's the sense of tragedy. It's more than lamentable that any individual would feel this way, let alone that so many do. It's heart-wrenching to know that some people are so far from love and acceptance that death seems to be the only solution. It's mind-boggling that trauma and chemistry can conspire in such death-dealing ways. It's also a reverberating pain for the loved ones—the survivors—of those who have taken their own lives.

If there is any God in this, I suspect it is this: suicide grieves God greatly. I believe that God is with us, feels with us, and is moved by our suffering—even when, especially when, we cannot feel God's presence.

I'm not sure the right word is "sin," but perhaps all of this breaks God's heart too.

~

Exploration
When have you felt abandoned by God?

Reflection
How can you remind yourself of God's presence?

Letting Others In

overlooked

Growing up in the Sunday school programs of black churches and in Catholic elementary school, I was taught that although there were many disciples, there were only twelve apostles. That is, there were many people who followed Jesus, but there were only twelve men whom Jesus handpicked to preach the gospel. These were the twelve men who were very close to Jesus, having been with him for the duration of his public ministry. I remember having to list them from memory in religion classes. They were the people in Jesus' inner circle.

But Acts 1:15-26 records something quite different. Peter makes a speech indicating that someone must be chosen to replace Judas as a member of the inner circle. By this time, Jesus has been crucified, buried, risen, returned, hung out with some disciples, and left again. The disciples are doing the last thing that Jesus told them to do—staying in the city and waiting for the power to come.

This is where we find out that there are about 120 disciples hanging out in the city, waiting for this power that Jesus promised. This is where we find out that there were at least two others —Barsabas and Matthias—who had been as active and present in

Jesus' ministry as the twelve men whose names I memorized for my elementary school religion tests.

Wait a minute! That means that there were anywhere from 14 to 120 people who had been with Jesus during his public ministry, even though history likes to record only 12. Only in verses like this one, or Luke 8:1-3, or the few mentions of Mary, Martha, and Mary of Magdala, do we get glimpses that there were others. There were women. There were other men.

Sadly, the tradition has overlooked the people who were right there with Jesus.

This story reminds me of how many people in my own life I overlook. And of how often I feel overlooked.

There is something isolating about living with a depressive condition. Sometimes that is because depression can be so physically and psychically crippling. Getting out of bed and leaving the house are monumental feats. Interacting with other people feels like an exertion of energy that cannot be mustered. And then what does one say to other people? "I feel sad. Just like I did yesterday, and the day before that and the month before that"? Not the most stimulating conversation.

The other isolation comes from stigma. A lot of people who live with depressive conditions are intensely private about their experiences. Even in an age when celebrities share experiences of depression and bipolar, and it's hard to watch a couple of hours of TV without seeing an ad for an antidepressant, there is still a lot of discrimination against people who share their condition. Employers, colleagues, and even friends may use knowledge of the condition against someone in professional and personal interactions.

Advocacy groups like the National Alliance for Mental Illness (NAMI), Depression and Bipolar Support Alliance (DBSA), and National Mental Health Association are working hard to tell the wider public that mental health challenges are physiological conditions that are managed—like diabetes. But anyone who lives with or loves someone who lives with a mental health challenge knows that this ad campaign has a lot more work to do.

Put together, listlessness and stigma push many people who live with mental health challenges into a silence that quickly becomes shame. When few people are talking about what they live with, it's easy to think you're all alone. When few people will share the struggles and triumphs they've found, it's hard to find other people with whom you can talk.

The irony is that community is the best antidote for isolation; acceptance is the best cure for silence and shame; fellowship is the best remedy for grief. I think Jesus knew this. He knew that his community was grieving. So he told them to stick together. If they spent enough time together, they would find their way forward. They would find each other. They would widen the circle.

When Peter was looking for a new number 12, he asked the disciples for a witness. In Acts 1:21, Peter says, "One of these must become a witness with us." African American church traditions have often asked for people who understood a certain experience in the same way:

Can I get a witness?

I have witnesses. I have friends who live with conditions similar to mine. We can talk about medicine and moods. We recognize states of wellness from the first hello. We can encourage each other by saying, "This sometimes works for me."

The funny thing is that I didn't really ask for them to be my witnesses. I shared something one day, and then my friend said, "Yeah, me too." Or my friend talked about something that sounded like a mental health challenge, and instead of letting it go, I asked to hear more and shared about mine. We are Barsabas and Matthias. We are here, just waiting to be asked to testify.

Other times I wonder how often I overlook members of my community who are like Barsabas and Matthias. How many times do I fail to trust my friends—who want to be there for me—with the truth of how I feel? How many times do I forget that I can call them when I need someone to sit with me or tell me a corny joke so I can laugh? When do I forget the people who care about me? I am still growing in this area.

In the biblical story of Christianity, this is when Spirit comes. When the community really sees and attends to one another, they are powerful enough to start a worldwide movement. And so are we.

~

Exploration
When have you felt overlooked?

Reflection
Who might you have overlooked?

community

For decades I've heard Barbra Streisand's voice crooning out words I know to be true: "People, people who need people, are the luckiest people in the world." Of course, I think that people needing people aren't just lucky; they're human. I think we all need other people. We all need community.

Religious folk like to call this "fellowship." In Christian traditions, we talk about the need for church. Thus, the season of Pentecost is about more than holy spirits and speaking in tongues. It is also about the beginning of the church. Acts 2:44-46 describes it succinctly:

> And all that believed were together, and had all things in common. And sold their possessions and goods, and parted them to all, as everyone had need. And they, continuing daily with one accord in the temple, and breaking bread from house to house, did eat their food with gladness and singleness of heart.

Every socialist bone in my body wants to declare this to be the appropriate model for church and society. But I can't claim that's the intent of the passage. What I see here is community as it should be: everyone has what she needs; there's a sense of spirituality, shared worship, good food, and good conversation.

It sounds simple, but anyone who has attended church or any place of worship in a religious tradition knows that it's not. This is not an indictment of what's wrong with today's religious communities. It's an acknowledgment that healthy community doesn't come easy or often.

I understand why people don't bother. Often enough, religious communities cultivate guilt and obedience, rather than spirituality. They elevate one worship style over another. Leadership is so hierarchical that there's little dialogue that's not gossip or complaint. Some places focus so heavily on spiritual needs that they forget hungry people cannot focus on holy text; they need real food. And then a good number of people don't get what they need spiritually. At least, these have been my experiences.

So I understand why people stop attending the organized fellowship of the traditions in which they were raised. I know why people gravitate toward individual spiritual practices and focus on their personal relationship with the divine. I can appreciate why someone would rather be "spiritual" than "religious."

There are times I wish I had that privilege. Yes, absenting from religious community does seem like a privilege to me. Sometimes I wish I could be satisfied with individual spiritual practice. I wish my private prayers to God fulfilled my spiritual needs. But as it turns out, I need drums and dance and spirituals and communal meals to feel God. I need community, even when I wish I didn't.

The other thing is that I can't afford it. Because depression is an isolating experience. It's far too easy to close the curtains, stay in bed, and stop talking to other people. Sometimes that occurs because the physical symptoms of depression lead that way. Other times, it's a defensive move, when one senses that people will not understand how one is truly feeling. And other times, all the energy one can muster has gone into the necessities of life—getting dressed, grocery shopping, going to work, raising the children—and there is nothing left for finding religious community.

Which for me is precisely why I must find community—even when I don't want to. I'm not sure whom I would turn into without it.

It's hard. It's really hard. I've moved across the country five times in the last decade. I've formed community and had to re-form it regularly (almost as soon as I found it and got settled in). Finding and building community requires some level of dedication. I go through a lot of communities and people who don't "click," before I find the community that does.

I like how the "How to Build Community" poster tells how us to do this:

> Turn off your TV. Leave your house. Know your neighbors. Look up when you are walking. Greet people. Sit on your stoop. Plant flowers. Use your library. Play together. Buy from local merchants. Share what you have. Help a lost dog. Take children to the park. Garden together. Support neighborhood schools. Fix it even if you didn't break it. Have pot lucks. Honor elders. Pick up litter. Read stories aloud. Dance in the street. Talk to the mail carrier. Listen to the birds. Put up a swing. Help carry something heavy. Barter for your goods. Start a tradition. Ask a question. Hire young people for odd jobs. Organize a block party. Bake extra and share. Ask for help when you need it. Open your shades. Sing together. Share your skills. Take back the night. Turn up the music. Turn down the music. Listen before you react to anger. Mediate

a conflict. Seek to understand. Learn from new and
uncomfortable angles. Know that no one is silent although many are not heard. Work to change this.

Overwhelming, right? I don't have to be a professional community
organizer (although I have been in the past). When it comes to
building community, the message I get is this: Pick one. It's a good
start.

This doesn't mean I always find the kind of community I crave:
people who understand me, or sit with me when they don't; who
love good food and music; who doesn't eschew God, change, or
difficulty; and who catch me when I fall, and let me do the same
for them.

The connection to Pentecost seems obvious: you don't get this
community without some kind of divine assistance.

∾

Exploration
Where have you found community?

Reflection
What idea from the "How to Build Community" poster
would you like to try to help you find community?

inertia

Physics was my most difficult class in high school. Every time the teacher posed a question and asked the class for an answer, I got it wrong. I did the equations and exercises and pushed around those little wooden carts, and I still never really got it. Even though I didn't get a good grade, I remained fascinated by the ideas of physics. I continue to be interested in concepts and theories about how the world works. (I now do that with philosophy or metaphysics.)

One of my favorite principles of classic Newtonian physics is the law of inertia. There are various ways of putting it, but it can be summarized in this way:

An object at rest tends to stay at rest.

I like this principle because it makes so much sense to me. It says that objects—and even people—don't change easily. It's also a scientific way of saying: things don't move. They stay in one place. Like a bump on a log. Inertia.

The concept of inertia accurately describes much of my everyday experience of living in a depression. I don't move. I stay in one place. Like a bump on a log. Or a bump on a couch. Inertia.

My mind doesn't turn off, but nothing really happens. There's a kind of physical paralysis that comes with depression. There's just no energy to do things, simple things like washing hair, making breakfast, packing school lunches. My internal dialogue goes something like this:

> *I have to do such and such. I really should do such and such. I don't feel like doing such and such. In fact, I'm really tired. I wonder if I can get back in the bed and throw the covers over my head and stay there for awhile. At least an hour or two longer. I should work out. But that would mean leaving the bed. Yes, I'll stay in the bed. I can probably go to work today. That would be okay. I guess. But I'm glad I don't have to go yet. God, this bed feels good.*

It's simply hard to find the energy and motivation to move.

There's a point in a depressive condition where something shifts downward. At one point, the healthy warrior tools work: exercise, certain foods, prayer, meditation, holistic health practitioners, massage, acupuncture. These things can keep someone healthy for a good stretch of time. They can even make a mild depression livable. But then, subtly—one missed workout, one comfort meal too many—something changes. One stops moving. Those tools seem like good ideas—good ideas, that is, for someone else who is able to move. Inertia sets in. At least, that's how it happens to me.

So I understand the biblical story about the man at the pool of Bethesda. It's found in John 5:1-18. As the story goes, there is this pool, and legend has it that at a certain time an angel will go into the pool and stir up the water. Whoever stepped into the water first after the angel stirred the water would be healed. So right by the pool, sick people gathered.

Crowds of sick, blind, injured, and paralyzed people gathered at the side of the pool waiting for something to happen. They waited for someone holy to stir things up. They waited for their change to come.

According to the story, Jesus interacts with one particular man who has had some kind of illness for thirty-eight years. When Jesus asks him if he wants to be well, he tells Jesus that he has no one to carry him into the pool when the water gets stirred up. Verses 6 and 7 read:

> When Jesus saw him lying there, and knew that he already had been in that condition a long time, He said to him, "Do you want to be made well?" The sick man answered Jesus, "Sir, I have no man to put me into the pool when the water is stirred up; but while I am coming, another steps down before me."

I can't count the number of sermons and Bible studies I've heard about how this man should have done something different. What kind of a person, they ask, can get so close to being healed but not get to it?

People who live with chronic health challenges can probably raise their hands in affirmation.

It's possible to *want* to be well but to be unable to get to the source of wellness. It's possible to be tired, run down, worn out, and paralyzed by the mere thought of having to move. It doesn't mean we don't want to be well. It doesn't mean we're lazy. It's inertia. It's hard to move.

I appreciate that the man in the Bible says that he needs someone to take him to the source of healing. He's saying that he cannot move on his own.

That reminds me of the rest of the law of inertia:

An object at rest tends to stay at rest,
unless an external force acts on it.

If an object is going to move, it's going to need some help from outside itself. Like the man at the pool of Bethesda, he needs someone to move him, to help him, to get him to the water.

I appreciate that Jesus was able to see that even if the man wasn't moving, he wanted to be well. I'm glad to have a story in which Jesus doesn't ask the man where his friends are or why he didn't scoot his way closer to the water. I'm glad to have a story in which no one tells the sick person to pray more diligently or find some kind of inner motivation. Jesus doesn't say, "Did you try…?" I like that Jesus comes to him. I like that Jesus recognizes inertia when he sees it.

Sometimes it takes an external force.

- A friend who drives you to the doctor and sits with you when they take blood.
- Someone to bring you dinner or order take out and watch TV with you while you munch together.
- A coworker who sees that you are tired and comes by the office to check in on you and drag you to that concert or lecture.
- A parent who takes the next flight out to make sure their grown child is going to make it to the next day.
- A friend who calls back because your "I'm okay" was completely unbelievable.

If there's any truth to Newton's laws and this Bible story, the external force doesn't have to be a miracle worker. Just someone who sees and knows to come and stir things up.

~

Exploration
When have you found yourself unable to move?

Reflection
What kind of external force is most helpful to you
when you can't move?

walk with me

One of America's protective freedoms lies in the principle of the separation of church and state. My friends who are legal scholars tell me that the provision was initially made to protect churches from the government. This "freedom of religion" means that the government will not persecute anyone for practicing her faith. It also means that the government will not coerce us all into practicing the same faith. This principle means that there are no government agents taking notes in our churches on Sundays, synagogues on Saturdays, mosques on Fridays, and so forth.

Sometimes, of course, we need to protect the government from religion. We need to ensure that arguments based on religious perspectives do not become the basis for our common laws. Rather, our laws should be based on the shared values of equality, freedom, justice, liberty, and that important but slippery phrase "the pursuit of happiness."

Over and over again, we see how difficult it is. *It is difficult to separate religion and politics.*

The field of liberation theology asserts that religious faith leads to political activism in the interest of justice. Liberation theology is an umbrella term of various theological expressions that situate the experiences of society's marginalized with the principles in religious texts that assert that we should treat each other the way we want to be treated, that God cares about the experiences of the outcast and downtrodden, and that our care for the oppressed in our midst reflects our love and devotion for God.

While this need not be a Christian principle, formal articulation of liberation theology was birthed in the late 1960s by Gustavo Gutiérrez in Peru, and James H. Cone in the United States. Gutiérrez was living and working among the poor in Latin America. Cone was considering the experiences of African Americans in the midst of the overturn of Jim Crow, assassinations, riots, the civil rights movement, and affirmation of self-love (black power). They both felt that the majority expressions of Christianity overlooked the Christianity that they read about in the Gospels:

> Luke 4:18: The Spirit of the Lord is upon me, because he hath anointed me to preach the gospel to the poor; he hath sent me to heal the brokenhearted, to preach deliverance to the captives, and recovering of sight to the blind, to set at liberty them that are bruised.

> Matthew 25:40: Truly I tell you, whatever you did for one of the least of these brothers and sisters of mine, you did for me.

They concluded that God has a preferential option for the poor (Gutiérrez) and that God is on the side of the oppressed (Cone).

In the last forty years, these ideas have developed into some pretty sophisticated and important theological movements, including Latin American, black, feminist, womanist, ecological, disability, and gay theologies. This is not an exhaustive list.

I have a lot of academic and historical reasons for calling myself a liberation theologian, but there are also intensely personal reasons as well. My faith motivates me to fight for justice. My religion inspires me to speak out for those who are often silenced or ignored. My relationship with God tells me that a primary form of worship involves standing against stigma, torture, and lack of equality. Sometimes that means I stand with governments who are doing the right thing. Often, it means standing against a powerful majority. That powerful majority can be found in groups of people or in institutions that wield power in oppressive ways.

I don't do this because I belong to one political party or another. While that motivates many humanists toward social justice, it would not be adequate motivation for me. I do this because it's what I believe in the depths of my spiritual understanding.

This is important because one common critique of liberation theology is that it tries to elevate one oppressed group over another, giving no role for those who are in the "oppressor" category. That would be a valid critique if it were true. Rather, liberation theologies acknowledge the power of our social locations and experiences in our understandings of God and the world. They may focus on the experience of one group but not to the exclusion of other forms of suffering in the world. Oppression is multivalent—an individual may be oppressed in one sense and privileged in another.

Liberation theologies call for us to acknowledge this. They call for us all to walk with those for whom equality, freedom, and justice is more of an ideal than a reality. I bring my understanding of liberation theology to my faithful struggle with depression.

People who live with depressive conditions experience a level of marginalization in today's society. We're called crazy. We're hard pressed to get health insurance that actually meets our needs. We're subject to sermons that suggest that greater faith would cure our depression (something I've never heard anyone say about diabetes or heart disease). We're negatively judged in most workplaces. We're told that a more positive outlook on life should make us happy inside and out.

Okay. It's not war. It's not torture. There are far worse things to be experienced—especially in developing and war-torn countries. Nevertheless, marginalization is still part of the daily experience of people who live with depressive conditions. And far too infrequently are we reminded that God loves us just as we are. And until we can feel that, someone else will stand with us and walk with us.

I'd like to think that it's ignorance, not true disdain, which leads to the many misunderstandings about depressive conditions that exist both within and outside of religious circles. I'd like to think that many people rarely think about the lives of those who live with depression from the inside. Or that perhaps, when they do, they do so out of pity, rather than with solidarity. That is, people with depressive conditions may be "one of the least of these." But they are also the people we all love. After all, everyone is just one life tragedy (such as the death of a loved one) away from a bout of situational depression. We are not such different people. Standing with us is standing for yourself.

This is a political act. It's a political act to stand with people who are suffering. It's a political act to hold the hand of someone you may not understand—while they are irritable, morose, negative, and weeping for no apparent reason. It's a political act to advocate for the things that would actually improve the lives of people with depressive conditions: universal health care, sufficient paid leaves from work, health coverage for preventative and nonpharmaceutical care. It's a political act to speak out against one's leaders and employers when they make prejudiced comments. It's a political act to question the parts of oneself that say and do things that trivialize the realities of people who live with mental health challenges. *Liberation theology says that these are political acts, but they are also deeply religious ones.*

When I feel isolated in this struggle, I hum this African American spiritual to myself over and over:

> *I want Jesus to walk with me*
> *I want Jesus to walk with me*
> *While I'm on this tedious journey*
> *I want Jesus to walk with me*
> *Walk with me Lord, walk with me*

Written by enslaved Africans in the United States and passed on orally to generations of both black Christians and freedom workers, this song has comforted and encouraged the brokenhearted and those harnessing their faith in the search for justice. It reminds me that God is walking with me—even when my journey feels difficult and tedious.

It also reminds me that, like freedom workers, there are people who care about the lives of people who live with mental health challenges. Here are some ways that people can walk with those of us who live with mental health challenges:

- Participate in your local NAMI Walks.
- Give the resources of Mental Health Ministries to your local faith leader.
- Preach about mental health during Mental Health Awareness Week (the first week in October).
- Financially support NAMI, DBSA, or NMHA.
- Challenge your religious leaders when they suggest that depression results from a lack of faith.
- Stand by your friends who live with depression even when they don't call back, haven't smiled in awhile, and can only think of what's wrong in the world.

- Make phone calls to health insurance agencies and doctors on behalf of a friend caught in an unhelpful medical system.

There's no checklist for the right thing to do. I listed things I know about and could often use in my life. Traveling with others is not about turning into a major activist—if that is not what God has called you to do. Walking with me and others who live with depressive conditions is also to walk with yourself. Some say it's also a walk with God.

The aboriginal Australian artist-activist-academic Lilla Watson put it best:

> If you have come here to help me, you are wasting your time. But if you have come because your liberation is bound up with mine, then let us work together.

~

Exploration
How can others walk with you?

Reflection
How does your faith motivate you to help others living with depressive conditions?

breaking bread

The disciples get a bad rap for not recognizing the risen Jesus. I've heard sermons about how we should not be like Thomas (John 20:24-29). We should not doubt. We should not need physical evidence. I've heard sermons about how we should not be like those men on the road to Emmaus (Luke 24:13-35). They could not see Jesus when he was in their midst. They didn't believe the scriptures would be fulfilled. These are examples of doubt. *We* should be pillars of faith.

Few people understand that doubt is a part of faith. I don't think anyone says it as beautifully as Paul Tillich in *Dynamics of Faith*:

> Many Christians, as well as members of other religious groups, feel anxiety, guilt and despair about what they call "loss of faith." But serious doubt is confirmation of faith. It indicates the seriousness of the concern, its unconditional character. . . . The criterion according to which they should judge themselves is the seriousness and ultimacy of their concern about the content of both their faith *and* their doubt.

I like that doubt, rather than about being an indication of a loss of faith, is presented as an indication that one takes one's faith seriously. One cares about one's faith enough to really investigate. Doubt is a good thing when it comes to our faith.

But I don't think the road to Emmaus is a story about faith and doubt. I think it's a story about friends and strangers.

The disciples don't recognize Jesus. They don't recognize their friend.

This speaks to me as someone who lives with depression. Depression runs a number on one's normal character. It takes something from you. Yes, it takes away sleep and appetite and happiness. At least, these are some of my symptoms. But it takes away more than that. It takes away energy to do basic things. It takes away vigor to accomplish necessary tasks. It changes how you see the world. It takes a piece of your soul. Spare moments surrender to lethargy. Pessimism is par. You try not to slip into desperation.

Who is this sad person who can't do anything?

Depression makes you someone else, someone other than who you know yourself to be. A shadow of another self. A self who, at one time, made friends and could speak in complete sentences. In its place, however, is a mere shell of that self. Yes, there are times when I barely recognize myself.

For some people, this is a season in time connected to a particular event. For others, it is part of the rhythm of life. Whether it happens once or multiple times, it transforms you. You can't get to the person you want to be. Depression can be like death.

Depressed people live close to death. Andrew Solomon says depression is like despair and grief to a higher degree. For those who have been suicidal, death is a dance partner. We know its moves better that we should.

I'm not saying that Jesus was depressed. I'm trying to say this: *Pain changes you.* Whether the risen Jesus had a transfigured body or a disabled one—as Nancy Eiesland argues—the risen Jesus was not the same Jesus who was crucified. When you know death so intimately and find by some miracle that you are still alive, nothing about you is the same as before. Of course the disciples didn't recognize Jesus, the one changed by death and resurrection.

What impresses me about the disciples is that they walked with a man they didn't recognize. He was a stranger, and they walked seven miles with him. He was a stranger, and they had a conversation with him. He was a stranger, and they invited him to a meal. I like these people who are willing to journey with a stranger. I like people who will walk with someone they don't recognize.

This is what I need most from my friends. When I'm this other depressed person, I need them to walk with me. I need them to talk with me. I need them to invite me to a meal. Because this is what brings me into new life. Ordinary companionship. It doesn't surprise me at all what moment it was when they recognized Jesus: during the breaking of bread.

∾

Exploration
How does pain change you?

Reflection
Who can walk with you when you don't recognize yourself?

to connect and to create

The camera pans to a living room. Dark hues mute an anguished woman's face as her body blends into the couch. Quiet, sentimental music crescendos. Voiceover: "Are you depressed?" One last shot at the blank, bleak face. Not two seconds later the world is Technicolor, the music upbeat. The woman runs in a field, flying a kite, her body bursting with energy. Her children run beside her.

The voiceover returns: "Depression hurts."

Little pills solve that problem.

Makes me want to throw my TV out the window.

There are a lot of things that bother me about these commercials. The thing that irks me today is the picture of depression. It's solved so easily. And so quickly. The woman is on the couch for ten, maybe fifteen seconds. Before you can reach for the remote, she's okay. No, not just okay—she's great!

I know they only have thirty seconds, but this image is worse than sit-coms that solve real problems in twenty-two minutes.

In real life, depression lacks drama and the simple arc of a hero's quest. That's why there aren't many movies about depression. There are a couple movies about psychiatric institutions (like *Girl, Interrupted*) and popular medicine (like *Prozac Nation*), but not about depression itself. When people go to make movies about mental health challenges, they make movies about people with schizophrenia or manias or dissociative identity disorder (what used to be called "multiple personality disorder"). Those are far more exciting. A lot more happens.

I think of depression as a time when things *don't* happen. If a movie showed what most of depression is like, it would focus on a person, on the couch, in the bed, with a remote control, watching the hours go by. Ennui lacks dramatic tension.

By its very nature, depression is isolating. Even if you're around other people, you can feel completely alone. More often than not, depressed folk don't want to be around other people. Because there's so little to say; it's so hard to explain. There's no clear, identifiable reason for the listlessness. Sometimes I want to be around other people, but I can't summon the energy to get dressed and leave the house. It cuts us off from the world.

If there is anything inherently evil about depression, this is it. Yes, evil. I'm loathe to use the words "evil" and "depression" in the same sentence, but I think it's appropriate here. If there is something to be fought in depression, it is the isolation. It is the seclusion. It is the way the mind turns in on itself to make one believe things that are not true: *You are completely alone.*

While I value my solitude and moments of contemplation, I think that the message behind the creation story of Genesis 2 underscores the words "It is not good for humans to be alone" (v. 18). My Hebrew scholar friends tell me that "good" does not connote moral assessment. Rather, when we read about creation and "goodness" in Genesis 1 and 2, it refers more to functionality.

> *Being alone is not good. It does not work. We do not function well on our own. We need community.*

And I don't think this is solely a Jewish and Christian thing. My Buddhist friend interprets the third of ten Buddhist precepts in the same way: "Our species has a drive passed down for thousands of generations to connect and to create."

We are called to connect and to create.

If you know Buddhism, you'll pause. The third precept is usually translated as "Abstain from sexuality." The Zen Center of Los Angeles translates it as "Do not be greedy. Do not misuse sex. Be respectful."

Likewise, Genesis continues with the edict to Adam and Eve in verse 22: "Be fruitful and multiply." These words are usually interpreted to promote heterosexual procreative, population-increasing sex. Whether you agree with that interpretation or not, I think it's noteworthy that the call to community is wrapped up in sex.

Sex is one way that we connect, and it is, especially to ancient peoples, a primary way that we create.

I read the message this way: Connecting creates. The ability to connect with other people, with ourselves, with our land, with our God has creative power. It creates community. It creates health. It creates change. It creates art. And in its optimal manifestations, whether procreative or recreative, sex connects. Sex strengthens bonds of intimacy (which is why there's a level of ironic cruelty in the fact that so many antidepressants diminish the sex drive).

I'm not suggesting people use sex to form all interpersonal connections. I'm not intimating that depression is solved by sexual intimacy. But I think that there is something as primal about the need for connection as there is about the human sex drive. And anything—including depression—that robs us of our capacity to connect and to create is against God's vision for our lives.

～

Exploration
What is one way that you connect with
other people when it's hard to do so?

Reflection
What can you communicate to others about
how to best reach out and connect to you?

unholy ghost

In the summer of 2002, I was a graduate student in religion who was tired of reading theology. In search of summer fiction, I walked into a large bookstore and stumbled into a book that hit closer to home than I ever could have imagined. There it was in the main display: *Unholy Ghost: Writers on Depression*.

Edited by Nell Casey, this volume contains essays from some of the most well-known memoirists on depression: Kay Redfield Jamison (*An Unquiet Mind*), Susanna Kaysen (*Girl, Interrupted*), William Styron (*Darkness Visible*), Meri Nana-Ama Danquah (*Willow Weep for Me*), Nancy Mairs (*Remembering the Bone House*), and Martha Manning (*Undercurrents*), to name a few.

These are writers with whom I was familiar, but it wasn't the roll call of authors that caught my attention. It was the title: *Unholy Ghost*. And the association of an unholy ghost with depression.

The title of the book is taken from a poem by Jane Kenyon, "Having It Out with Melancholy," which contains a section called "Credo" that's worth citing here:

Pharmaceutical wonders are at work
but I believe only in this moment
of well-being. Unholy ghost,
you are certain to come again.

Coarse, mean, you'll put your feet
on the coffee table, lean back,
and turn me into someone who can't
take the trouble to speak; someone
who can't sleep, or who does nothing
but sleep; can't read, or call
for an appointment for help.

There is nothing I can do
against your coming.
When I awake, I am still with thee.

As someone who clings closely to God, Spirit, and religion, yet
also has intimate experience with depressions, I was fascinated that
depression would be so closely associated with an "unholy ghost."
And then I noticed. It's not just Jane Kenyon and Nell Casey.
When writers begin to talk about the experiences of mental health
challenges, they talk about demon possession.

Yes, the therapist was wonderful, they report. And the medication, through trial and error, with side effects and expense, is ir-
replaceable. But no matter how you slice it, National Book Award
winner Andrew Solomon says that he is still stalked by a "noonday
demon," the title of his award-winning book, subtitled *An Atlas of
Depression.*

Listen to the language: "ghost," "demon," "unholy," "coming,"
"stalking," "taking over," "turning me into someone else."

I understand completely. If grief can make people act out-of-sorts, depression can make a person feel entirely displaced. In the midst of depression, it seems reasonable to ask oneself, "Who is this person who is so sad? Who is this person who can't get out of bed? Who is this person who can't hold a complete thought?" I look in the mirror, and it's the same body. But something inside is different. It *is* like spirit possession.

And it's not good. Pain blots out all happiness. Sleep is a stranger. Going to work is like climbing Mt. Everest. Death seems preferable to numbness. It's misery. My colleague Kathleen Greider calls it "soul suffering." I can see why someone would call it an unholy ghost.

But does it have to be an *unholy* ghost?

For people like me who live with bipolar depressions, there is a flip side. There is also great exuberance and joy. There is supreme confidence and ability. Even when the effects can be destructive, it *feels* very good. If this is spirit possession, it is Casper, the Friendly Ghost.

I feel torn. I understand that some traditions talk about demons and ghosts that haunt and torture. That's everywhere from *Scooby-Doo* cartoons to *Ghost Whisperer*. This seems an apt metaphor for a debilitating, often recurring, sadness that diminishes life.

But faith traditions also talk about the possession of spirits: holy spirits. Holy spirits don't come to taunt and torture. In my Pentecostal and neo-Pentecostal Christian experiences, the Holy Ghost comes with a prophecy. An individual may speak in tongues. And if you are in community, and you wait, the interpretation will come. Paul talks about this in 1 Corinthians 12:1-10.

In the religion of the Yoruba peoples of southwest Nigeria, certain orisha (ancestor spirits) possess as well. Then an individual takes on all the characteristics of the orisha—which are quite different from what that person would normally do. The orisha comes to give the community a message as well.

Both traditions agree that spirit possession is tiring. When it's over, the person needs care. She may fall over. He will need to be fanned. She will need water. He will need rest. The community is there. They know what to do. They have towels, white cloths, water, places to lie down. This is not so abnormal to them. It's part of what it means to be spiritual.

It's hard to think about depression as a messenger. It's hard to think that there is something I am supposed to know or learn—or that others should know or learn—from my depression. I've always been loathe to say that we suffer in order to learn or grow. It's *nice* when we can grow or learn *after* experiences of suffering, but generally speaking, suffering sucks.

Sometimes, weeks or months or years after a depression (with a lot of help from a therapist or spiritual guide), I can see a lesson. In the depression, I remembered something important I had forgotten. Or I found a new part of myself. Or I learned new skills for operating in the world. But that never eases the pain at the time. I am blinded to any fable-like moral. I have no time for reflection—I'm just surviving in the limbo that is depression.

I think it's a worthy idea. Perhaps depression can be a friendly spirit, a holy ghost. Perhaps there is a message or a lesson. I'm not sure. What I do understand from Pentecostalism and Yoruba religion is that spirit possession and depression are exhausting. And it's nice when there are people around who will interpret, catch you, fan you, offer water and rest. And that's just normal for them.

≈

Exploration
Have you ever learned something new about
yourself or the world after a depression?

Reflection
Who can offer you rest when you are exhausted?

Touching Love,
Beauty, and Joy

ordinary time

I first read the book *Siddhartha* by Hermann Hesse in high school. This short novel describes the spiritual journey of a boy in India. The protagonist, Siddhartha, leaves home in search of enlightenment. His life involves asceticism, wealthy business trade, love, and finally a humble occupation as a ferryman. It was years before I understood that this is a story of the Buddha. I was not attracted by the book's spirituality. I was attracted to Hesse's description of Siddhartha's journey.

Although Siddhartha is passionate in his seeking, Hesse's story is also patient. Siddhartha's journey begins in boyhood and ends when he is an old man. Each stage of his life takes years and years. In every phase, Siddhartha is fully committed to the life that he is leading. He is unable to anticipate where life will take him next, and yet he embraces the next place he finds himself.

That impresses me. It impresses me because that kind of patience, commitment, and acceptance are rare. It's easier to live in extremes. It's easier to live for the momentous occasions. In Hesse's *Siddhartha*, there are few exciting moments or action scenes. Siddhartha's philosophical and spiritual insights are the jewels of the book. The dramatic tension does not come from a sensational incident that, if turned into a movie with an A-list actor, could make a blockbuster film.

Rather this book always reminds me of the importance of ordinary time. I find this particularly relevant as one who lives with a bipolar depressive condition. The terminology of "polar" connotes opposite tendencies. This is supposed to be an improvement over previous language of "manic depression"—the term that described what the poles were. The language seems to imply that one is either one thing or the other, that one lives at the extreme ends of mood and behavior.

When I hear that, I imagine a pendulum swinging back and forth, from one mood to the other.

In my experience, there's a long arc from one pole to another. Most of my life is lived there. In the arc. It's not particularly exciting or noteworthy. I'm not superwoman, nor am I in the depths of sadness. I'm a person who gets up, gets dressed, and goes to work. It's fairly ordinary.

In a Christian liturgical calendar, the season called "ordinary time" is the longest. The high holy days of Christian calendars focus on the birth and death of Jesus, and then the birth of the church: Advent, Epiphany, Lent, Easter, Pentecost. Then there are nearly seven months of "ordinary time." During this time, Christians are encouraged to focus on the life and ministry of Jesus.

It's a good idea, but it's difficult to remember when so much energy and excitement are given to birth and death. It leads one to think that what is important about Jesus is who he is—that he was born a certain way for a certain purpose and that he could live after dying. It takes away an emphasis on what Jesus did and taught and how he lived, which are far more fascinating to me. But those parts of his life are also longer and more ordinary. So ordinary, in fact, that the canonical Gospels leave out descriptions of most of Jesus' life.

Life spent in ordinary time is important. This is when I learn to put one foot in front of the other. I establish healthy habits that I can draw on when I find myself at an extreme. I make friends. I love. I practice hope and trust. Sometimes I sit still. This is what I saw in *Siddhartha* and what I experience in my ordinary moments.

It's taken me time to appreciate these places. I was taught to be ambitious and driven, to have goals, and to celebrate their attainment—and then to be about the business of setting new goals. But one cannot live there all the time. Ordinary time says that it's okay to be ordinary. It's okay to live, learn, eat, love, and pray. Those are ends in themselves.

After the long and ordinary life of searching for enlightenment, Hesse describes one of Siddhartha's dramatic insights in this way:

> When someone is seeking . . . it happens quite easily
> that he only sees the thing that he is seeking; that he is
> unable to find anything, unable to absorb anything . . .
> because he is obsessed with his goal. Seeking means:
> to have a goal; but finding means: to be free, to be
> receptive, to have no goal.

What's nice about ordinary time is that one can stop living at the limits and can even stop focusing on the goal. One can savor the process. There is joy just in the journey.

The Christian singer Michael Card expresses this well in his short song "Joy in the Journey":

> *There is a joy in the journey*
> *There's a light we can love on the way*
> *There is a wonder and wildness to life*
> *And freedom for those who obey*

Both Card and Hesse suggest that when we live fully where we are, embrace the ordinary, and find joy in the journey, we will find what we've been looking for. And we will be free. And it is holy.

∾

Exploration
What are you doing in the ordinary times of your life?

Reflection
Where is there joy in your journey?

laughter

"Jesus wept."

This is the famously simple biblical verse that the first kid spouts off in the Vacation Bible School lineup of children demonstrating that they have memorized at least one Bible verse. It's short. It commits well to memory. And it leaves every other kid reaching into his or her mental arsenal for another verse to recite.

"Jesus wept."

It's the shortest verse in the King James Version of the Bible, and its true value is that it reveals Jesus' humanity—something not often emphasized in the Gospel of John. After Lazarus's death and in the face of Mary and Martha's deep grief, Jesus wept (John 11:35).

"Jesus wept."

It reminds us that Jesus was made of the same stuff as the rest of us. We can debate his divinity all day and night, but Jesus was at least human. He cried. He ate. He worked. Presumably he put on his pants one leg at a time.

It has only now occurred to me that in all the biblical expressions of Jesus' humanity, we never see reports of Jesus laughing. We know he went to dinner parties. We know he celebrated feast days.

He went to a wedding. He had friends. We can assume he laughed, but we never get a recording of it.

Jesus is usually pictured as a pretty somber guy. Think of the picture of the Last Supper that you've seen. Jesus with all his friends. He's looking profound. Sad. Really wise and holy. Or stoic. But he doesn't look the way I do when I'm having dinner with my friends: laughing and having a good time.

The importance of laughter has really hit home lately. I found myself laughing as I read a couple pages of Therese Borchard's book *Beyond Blue: Surviving Depression & Anxiety and Making the Most of Bad Genes*. I didn't just chuckle. I laughed. I laughed hard. I interrupted the people sitting around me in the coffee shop. I almost blew water out of my nose. It was funny.

What, one might reasonably ask, can be that funny in a memoir about depression?

I laughed because I really identified with the passage I read. And Borchard has a great, wry sense of humor. She's able to describe really challenging life events with a slightly self-deprecating distance and wit that keeps one from feeling depressed while one is reading about depression.

My laughter also reminded me of the importance of laughter in the context of depression. For me, the absence of laughter is a true-tell sign that I'm depressed. Here's how it happens: One day, something will be funny. Not the kind of funny where you get the joke and smile and nod your head. Not the kind of funny where you giggle a little bit. The kind of funny where you lean your head back and ignore whatever sound is coming out of your mouth. And then I'll hear myself think (sometimes I say it out loud): "I can't remember the last time I laughed."

I can't. I will be unable to remember the last time I laughed. That means it has been weeks or months since I've really laughed. That means, I haven't been happy in a long time. Of course, the laughter also means I'm feeling a little better now.

The laughter surprises me because it's fairly easy to go around not laughing. I can smile and do my job quite well. There's no expectation that a professor and minister should be laughing. To the contrary—religion is generally supposed to be a really serious topic. I talk about matters of spiritual life and death. I preach about salvation and ethics. I teach about theory and philosophy. Sober material.

Christian traditions don't emphasize laughter very much. Some religious traditions are better at this. For example, Buddhism has an enviable image of a laughing Buddha. Some traditions have strong trickster figures that often laugh and delight (sometimes at someone else's lack of wisdom). Western Christianity—well, not so much. Western Christians may talk about having joy, but we don't have many images or pictures of laughter.

Jesus didn't laugh.

I've missed it myself. In my book *Making a Way Out of No Way: A Womanist Theology*, I talk about the various experiences and charges of a Savior. I am careful to note that a Savior's work can be challenging and difficult. Why do you think Jesus needed to get away by himself every once in awhile? This salvation business is hard.

I forgot to say that the work of salvation can also be fun. I forgot to say how important it is to have not just disciples, but also friends. This is something the Gospel of John emphasizes a lot (chapters 13–16). I forgot to say that sometimes we professional religion folk get together and laugh our heads off over the funny things we encounter. I think I forgot this because it's easy to forget. It's easy to get caught up in how important and serious and life-changing something is, and forget to take a break and laugh.

So I think we have to be intentional about getting the laughter in. I'll rent and re-rent the same DVD by my favorite comedian. It's guaranteed to put me in stitches.

I do this because I know that laughter is good for me. Literally. Laughter kicks in all types of chemicals that are known to ease depression—like beta-endorphins. Scientists actually document this. Therese Borchard summarizes nine ways humor heals. Here are a couple of things laughter and humor do:

1. Combat fear
2. Comfort
3. Reduce pain
4. Boost the immune system
5. Reduce stress

This reminds me of how amazing and complex the human body is. It makes me think about how God creates us with some ability to heal ourselves. It reminds me that laughter is a gift from God.

I might have arrived here sooner if one of the Gospels had a verse saying, "Jesus laughed." Without that, I've become content with this quote from the writer Anne Lamott: "Laughter is carbonated holiness."

Yeah, it is.

～

Exploration
What do you think about holiness?

Reflection
What can you do to laugh more?

one of us?

The headline in the electronic newsletter appeared in large font: "SHE'S ONE OF US." My favorite magazine that offers hope and harmony to people living with bipolar depressions, *bphope*, called attention to the recent disclosure that actress Catherine Zeta-Jones lives with bipolar depression. By the time I received the newsletter, I had already read a lot about Zeta-Jones on my Twitter feed, in the *Huffington Post*, and on the cover of magazines in the grocery store checkout.

Even though I live in Los Angeles, where people are often defined by their relationship to "the industry" (Hollywood and all the support the movie and television business incur), I have never been swept up in celebrity news. In fact, I find it hard to understand why some people are so interested in the personal lives of other people who are known primarily through their portrayal of fictional characters.

This headline helped me understand.

She's one of us.

Someone out there, someone big, someone gorgeous and rich and famous is not so far away. She's not so different from regular people. In fact, she's one of *us*.

Although contemporary medicine and mainstream media have done a lot to let the public know that living with a depressive condition is analogous to living with any other chronic medical condition, there is still a significant stigma to living with a depressive condition.

Most people still know bipolar as "manic depression" and have an image of someone with tremendous mood swings—from grandiose superhuman feeling highs to sullen poutiness.

Most people still use terms like "crazy," "insane," and "nut job" in flippant and careless ways when they would not use comparable terms about physical challenges, sexuality, or race.

Most people do not think of the complex causes of depressive conditions—some unknown cocktail of family history, environment, body chemistry, and life circumstances. Nor do they realize what everyday machinations are required to stay healthy.

Most people I know who live with depressive conditions spend a good amount of time hiding them or weighing the advantages and consequences of sharing the fact of their conditions with employers or loved ones. Because we don't want to be blamed, excused, or treated differently because we live with a depressive condition.

So when someone well known—and presumably well liked—is revealed as one of *us*, it makes a difference. It makes living with a bipolar depressive condition seem more commonplace. It shows that there are talented, gorgeous, famous people who live with depressive conditions. It shows that having a bipolar depressive condition does not close off the possibility of being glamorous, talented, admired, or famous. It widens the circle of "insiders," so that we begin to hope that one day we might stop drawing lines between who is in and who is out of what is normal.

We aren't so unusual.

She's one of us.

In the season of high holy days in Christian traditions, people focus a lot on what makes Jesus exceptional. Some traditions talk about his birth to a virgin woman. By the time we get to holy week, we talk about how Jesus conquers death. Various Christian communities will talk about Jesus' ability to forgive when betrayed; Jesus' ability to bestow a life in paradise; Jesus' ability to rise from the dead; Jesus' ability to save us from sin and death.

All of this is because Jesus is *not* like us. Because, some interpretations assert, Jesus is a mystical combination of full divinity and full humanity. Jesus was human but did not sin. Jesus has a special relationship with God (think "only begotten son"). This is why Jesus can save us. Because, as the early Christian thinker Athanasius often put it, "Only God can save."

Another early Christian thinker, Gregory of Nazianzus, asserted the opposite. He felt that "What is not assumed cannot be healed." Only a human can save humanity. Part of what makes Jesus so exciting is that he is human.

I hear the headline again.

Jesus is one of us.

Jesus had parents. Jesus walked. Jesus wept. Jesus ate. Jesus struggled. Jesus prayed. Jesus had friends. Jesus was betrayed. Jesus had some things to say. Jesus got tired. Jesus was killed.

Just like finding out that a celebrity—who is widely admired—shares something with those of us whom society often maligns, Jesus' humanity is encouraging. It means that someone who is admired, respected, uplifted, and worshipped is just like us.

It also means that we, too, may do the things we see as exceptional about Jesus: we can forgive, seek ideals in our communities, stand up for justice, welcome the ostracized, see life overpower death, and pursue healing for the world.

The Easter message is brought to us by words from a pop song: God is one of us.

~

Exploration
What parts of Jesus' humanity do you connect with?

Reflection
Where do you see God in others?

getting happy

I make grits on weekend mornings. Eating grits on the weekends reminds me of leisurely family breakfasts with my parents, talking about nothing important, not having to rush to school or work or any place of consequence. Since we were the only people in Michigan I knew who ate grits, and we were the only black people in my neighborhood, I assumed that grits were a black cultural thing.

Imagine my surprise when I was exposed to white Southerners who also ate grits. As it turns out, grits are a Southern thing. When I mentioned this to my mother, she laughed. "Well," she said, "all black people are Southern."

Of course this isn't completely true. There are generations of African Americans in New England and Canada. And there are generations of black folk in America who trace their roots to specific African and Caribbean societies.

My mother was referring to the profound legacy of the U.S. slavery system, how entrenched it was in the southeastern United States, how black and white peoples were so intermingled—even in their inequality—that they share some cultural markers. So when these black people, like my grandparents, migrated north, they were still Southern inside.

I later learned about what students of African American history refer to as "the great migration." Between 1910 and 1930, when factory and government jobs opened up in the North, and there seemed to be an escape from the Jim and Jane Crowism of the south, almost two million African Americans left their Southern homes: along the railroad lines between Jackson, Mississippi, to Memphis, Chicago, and Detroit; westward from Texas and Arkansas and Oklahoma to Kansas and California; and up the eastern seaboard to Philadelphia, DC, and Baltimore. My grandparents were in the latter group. They were all looking for a better life, a "promised land."

So I spent my summers in DC with my grandparents, in the same way many Northern-living African Americans sent their children "down South." These extended trips allowed me to spend time with my grandparents and cousins. They also allowed me to experience a cultural environment that was not found in the Midwestern semirural town where I grew up.

It was in this environment where I first saw someone filled with the Holy Spirit.

I could not have been even ten years old. I was at a Sunday worship service at Shiloh Baptist Church in Washington, DC. Not too far from us, a woman started shouting. She threw up her arms, her fancy hat careening to the side. She thrashed her arms and her legs and shouted and screamed. She even danced a little bit. It wasn't like the dancers on *Dance Fever*, but it was a dance.

I asked my grandmother what was happening, and she said, "She's getting happy."

I accepted Grandma's answer, while I continued to stare. A moment ago, she had been sitting quietly in the pew, and now she was ecstatically—and disruptively, it seemed to me then—happy?

I couldn't help but wonder: *What could make her so happy?*

Perhaps the woman was meditating on how amazing God had been in her life. Perhaps she was thinking about all the difficulties she had experienced and how God had played a part in the fact that she was surviving them, or even on the other side of them. That's what Grandma later said.

The womanist sociologist of religion Cheryl Townsend Gilkes goes further. She says that in African American churches where people have charismatic experiences of Spirit, the church functions as a therapeutic community. Here "blacks are able to act-out and work-through whatever happens to be troubling them." Gilkes notes that other members "become therapists for their fellow church members in that they attend to their shouting, encourage them in their feelings and guard and protect them from possible harm." Perhaps this woman wasn't happy, but she knew that she had a safe space to express her emotions—and that would ultimately make her happy.

As a minister, I try to remember that I rarely know the experience each person brings to church. I don't know what someone's week or month or year has been like. I don't know the level of loss or grief someone's known. I don't know the triumphs and blessings a person has had, either. But I like the fact that I may get to be part of a space where someone connects her experiences to community, safety, and Spirit. I like that Grandma looked at all this and said, "She's getting happy."

As someone who lives with depression, I know how to appreciate happiness. I can go months without feeling "happy." I can live through these places. I can cook and clean and work and love and take children to school without being happy. In those seasons, I can't even remember what it feels like to be happy. I'll know that I once was happy, but it's like looking at someone else's life on a video.

Since I live with a bipolar form of depression, I can also know great happiness. I can feel so good that I can't remember what it feels like to be sad. I know that I have been sad, but *that* is like looking at someone else's life. I can dance and work and read and write and be social and learn new things and be proficient at old things, and do this all before sunset. It's like this for months on end.

Unlike what Cheryl Townsend Gilkes describes, I'm not working anything out. For me, the happiness is a flip side of working through more difficult times. Because there are patterns in my moods, I know that if I hold on through a depression, I will feel happy.

Joy is a reward for surviving.

Perhaps this is what I share with those filled with the Holy Spirit. In ecstatic expression, they convey that it can be miraculous to live through things that kill people. The shouts say that only God could know where we've been and provide hope that there is somewhere better. The dance says that no matter what the previous week or months were like, today I am happy.

This is spiritual and therapeutic hope for me, and I thank my family for teaching me this at an early age.

≈

Exploration
How do you demonstrate the feeling of happiness?

Reflection
How can you reward yourself for surviving?

fully human

"What does it mean to be a human being?" This is one of those questions I heard in the opening lecture to the required philosophy class in college. It was the kind of thing that made me hate philosophy. I wasn't interested in hearing historical and contemporary postulations about something that could not really be answered.

Of course, philosophy does not monopolize the market to this question. In some sense, most academic fields have responses. There are anthropological and sociological responses that discuss how human beings relate to one another—distinctly from how other animals do. There are biological responses, which become political when measured in debates on things like reproductive rights and abortion. And there are theological responses that talk about things like having a soul, being created by divinity, possessing the "breath of God," and having a purpose.

The fact that I'm a professional theologian suggests that I prefer to wrestle with the religious answers to this question. I believe I have a soul or spirit that will outlive my physical body. I believe that God created me and has a hand in my ongoing development and growth. I believe that God is deeply inside of me, in every breath and every cell—while also being much bigger than I can imagine.

And I believe that God calls me to help make the world a better place using my gifts and talents. These ideas ground me, but I'm not sure they make me human.

I also think that many religions often downplay what it means to be human. There can be such an intense focus on spirit and transcendence and nirvana and perfection and holiness that our humanity can get lost in translation. In Christianity, we are often so focused on the idea that Jesus is "fully divine" that we lose the power of how amazing it is that Jesus is a lot like us: "fully human."

This week, I was reminded that humanity simply feels like *life* to me. I was riding my bicycle and said to myself—almost aloud— *I feel human again.*

Cycling makes me feel whole and clear and sane. Having learned to ride a bike later in life (in my teens, then forgetting, and again in my late twenties), I'm proud of the fact that I'm actually not falling over. I can feel my mind connect with my body and spirit. I can feel the breeze on my face and the sun on my arms. I mean it exactly the way I thought about it on that day: cycling is one of those things that restores my humanity.

It's entirely possible that my depressed neural system simply needs an infusion of endorphins every day. And my cells appreciate the additional oxygen from aerobic breathing. I don't deny that. But that's not how I feel it.

I feel that there are things that eat away at my humanity. Every day. Long meetings, violence on television, sitting in a traffic jam, fighting racism and sexism, fussing at children. Those are just a few of the things. They operate so slowly and surreptitiously that I don't even realize how bad I feel until I get on my bike and feel life infused into my pores once again.

My humanity seems to be on some kind of sliding scale from −10 to +10. There are things that move me along the scale. Of course, I need the things that keep me on the positive side. They give me life. They keep me alive. Cycling is one of them. Cooking is another. (I've actually given an entire lecture on how baking and biking serve as spiritual disciplines in the context of depression.) I have friends who say the same things about walking or yoga or making pottery.

My hobbies are my lifelines.

They are the things that connect me to God, my self, my spirit, my body, and the world outside of me. In especially difficult seasons, they are the only things that curb the lifeless numb feeling—which is like falling off the ten-to-ten scale. Sometimes I get resentful that these things are not optional for me. I don't do certain things just for fun. I do them because I need them to feel human.

I hope that the second-century bishop Irenaeus was correct when he wrote the following words (adapted for inclusivity):

> The glory of God is humanity fully alive,
> And the life of humanity is the vision of God.

If he's right, the things that I do—that I assume we all must do—to be well and to feel and to have life are not just survival skills in a kit we acquire over time. Rather, the whirl of the tires, looking out for traffic, the tough uphill climbs, and the glorious moments of cruising downwards are actually worship.

~

Exploration
What are some of your survival skills?

Reflection
What makes you feel alive?

gratitude

The American holiday of *Thanksgiving* kicks off a season when a spirit of gratitude pervades society. From the media to faith communities, the notion of thankfulness abounds.

I've always found it problematic that the value of gratitude is so closely tied to an American myth of cooperation. Most school children are taught that Pilgrims, an English Puritan sect of Calvinism escaping religious persecution, were welcomed to the northeastern coast of what is now the United States of America by the local Native Americans, the Wampanoags. The Wampanoags helped the Pilgrims survive their first winter, teaching them how to live off the land. During the next year, the Puritans shared their first harvest with the Wampanoags.

This part of the story is shared by both the wider American public and the Wampanoags. The difference comes in interpretation. This sharing of food and resources represented a friendship of exchange. It signals gratitude and the value of breaking bread together.

But I see this as a landmark event that revealed the differences between how many Europeans and most Native Americans understand land. It was also a symbolic beginning of the genocide of Native Americans under the rubric of manifest destiny, fueled by an appropriation of the Hebrew Bible's exodus narrative of expansion (and conquer) into the land of milk and honey that God promised. It also exhibits a centuries-old global trend where a newly freed oppressed people go on to oppress another community.

Every liberationist and Cherokee bone in my body resists being thankful for this. I do, however, understand that this story is used as a launching pad for emphasizing gratitude. For some people, that involves large meals with family and noting the past year's highlights. Other people make a list of their blessings. In my black church tradition, we go to church and have a testimony service when anyone in the congregation can stand and share how God has blessed him or her in the last year. It often begins this way: "Giving honor and glory to God who is the head of my life, I just want to thank God for . . ."

As a person who lives with depression, I find Thanksgiving to be a particularly difficult time. I know many people experience depressions during these times because they miss family members who have passed on. Other people struggle with the waning sun and short and dark days of the season. That's not my challenge. The challenge for me has always been the expression of gratitude.

When I'm in a depression, I don't exude joy. I don't know that I *exude* anything. I'm lucky if I can feel anything but bad. As winter approaches, I have to work hard to avoid the numbness that depressions can bring.

For me, gratitude is an intellectual knowledge, but it is not a feeling. That is, I can be thankful without seeming thankful. I may even appear mopey. This does not impede my ability to know that there is good in the world and good in my life. It just doesn't translate to my face, tones, or movements.

It seems as if I'm not grateful at all, when the opposite is true. People who live with depressive conditions live closer to death and dismay than most people outside our internal thoughts could ever know. It's not a daily threat most of the time, but it is a reality, and for many of us, it's recurrent. For this reason, we are deeply grateful that the next day has come and we can start over again. We are thankful that we lived through the last bout. We appreciate that we have outlasted this thing within and outside of us that sometimes threatens our very existence. At least, this is the case for me and some of my friends.

There is one religious writer who expresses this extraordinarily well. He survived the Jewish Holocaust or Shoah. He was sent to Nazi German concentration camps and made it out. He saw friends and family killed; he even witnessed his father's murder. As he becomes increasingly disillusioned with humanity and God, Elie Wiesel pens these words in his book *Night*:

> No one is as capable of gratitude as one who has
> emerged from the kingdom of night.

It's not the "kingdom of night" that engenders thanks. It's the emergence. Sometimes depressions obscure the possibility of emergence. Depression can twist my mind and emotions so that all I can feel is the "kingdom of night." But I know that I've emerged before, and it can happen again.

I believe that God doesn't care if I exude, bow, stand, or share my thanks with anyone. God knows how much energy it takes to stay in the flow of life—working, cooking, gathering, eating, and cleaning. And, in my faith, it's God who facilitates whatever emergence happens. Even when I can't feel that, I believe it in the core of who I am. And for that, I am most thankful.

~

Exploration
When do you find it difficult to "feel" gratitude?

Reflection
For what "small things" are you grateful?

Knowing
Yourself as
Complete
and Whole

the right question

"Are you sure, sweetheart, that you want to be made well?"

These are the opening lines of Toni Cade Bambara's amazing novel *The Salt Eaters*. Black faith healer Minnie Ransom leads a community of friends and clinicians who respond to Velma Henry's attempted suicide.

On the next page, the healer Minnie expounds: "I like to caution folks, that's all. No sense us wasting each other's time."

On the third page, the healer continues, "A lot of weight when you're well. Now, you just hold that thought."

The Gospels portray Jesus with the same prodding—but with more brevity. Before a healing miracle, Jesus asks the man who has been sick for thirty-eight years, "Do you want to be made whole?" (John 5:6). Some biblical translations write this way:

Do you want to be made well?

I like this question for all that's behind it.

The healers are asking: Are you willing to have a new experience?

You know sickness, but you don't know wellness. You've learned how to manage what you do know. You know it like the back of your hand. You know how it dips, turns, and immobilizes. You know the hint that today is a bad day. You know how to hide it, work through it, or surrender to it. (At least I do.) So are you willing to venture into the unknown? Are you ready to learn new ways of being in the world? Are you willing to trade a familiar sickness for a health you may not recognize? Are you willing to feel things you haven't felt before? That's a lot of weight. Are you sure you want to be made well?

The healers are asking: Are you willing to work for it?

The road from sick A to well B is not straight or paved. It winds; there are obstacles; you will fall on the path. Are you willing to get back up again? And again? You will feel as if you are groping in the dark. Will you trust that there is light at the end? Until you get there, can you work with the shadows? You will need community. Can you trust those who love you? Can you hold tight with one hand and release with the other? You will have to trust in the process. You will need faith. Do you want to be made well?

These are real questions for people who live with chronic conditions like Bambara's Velma, the Gospel's sick man, and those of us who live with mental health challenges. Of course one wants to feel better. But are we willing to have new experiences? Are we willing to work for it? Do we want it *bad enough*?

Getting to "yes" is a journey all its own. It's a big deal to crave wellness more than the comfort of what is well known and in the face of the trial-and-error character of the work. It takes many of us years to excavate the hope that is needed to walk the way to wellness. That should be enough.

Do you want to be made well?

I like this question for all that's behind it. I also like this question for all that it's not. It's not:

Why are you here?
What's wrong?
What are your symptoms?
Do you have health insurance?

I suspect that contemporary healers want to be like Minnie and Jesus. They don't want their first questions to be clinical and financial. They don't want to identify people by what they've done or how they've felt. They don't want to come up with labels so that they know how to bill people. I suspect that they want to assure people they can be well. I think healers want to hold hands along the way. I imagine healers want to do what works. I suspect that contemporary healers even crave the confidence of Minnie and Jesus: if you want to be well, I can help you get there.

This is one of the reasons why I support universal health care and think all people of faith should as well. Because it's hard to live with deep pain and still say, "Yes, I'm willing to embark on what is uncertain. Yes, I'm willing to work. Yes, I believe."

I want a society where *that's* the hard work. Not the paperwork. Not the fear of a diagnosis because it will kill your chances of getting individual health coverage, let alone life insurance. Not avoiding doctors because you can't afford them. Not telling your secrets to someone you don't trust because the therapist you like doesn't take insurance. Not taking a death-dealing job for health benefits with pitiful mental health coverage. Not finally finding the right medication and realizing that it costs $400 a month because insurance only covers generic and that doesn't work.

When you're trying to heal, you shouldn't have to worry about these kinds of things.

I want a society where the healers ask the only question they need to know the answer to: *Do you want to be made well?*

~

Exploration
Do you want to be made well?

Reflection
Are you ready for the unknown? Are you willing to work for it?

crutches

I own a pair of crutches. I keep them in the hallway closet where I can grab them if I need them—because every so often I will. I have a knee condition in which my kneecaps naturally dislocate. I can move my kneecaps with my hand, or they will naturally dislocate in a regular rhythmic way. It doesn't hurt. But when my kneecap dislocates outside of that rhythm, I collapse. I fall to the ground, grasping my knee, shouting expletives as tears come to my eyes.

My kneecap will move back into place automatically, but the unexpected offbeat shift is painful. It is then that I use crutches. The crutches don't prevent my kneecap from dislocating. The crutches let my knee rest so it can heal.

It took me years to understand this.

I was eight years old when I first learned of this condition. The orthopedic surgeon told me that nothing could be done to cure me. Surgery would not significantly change anything. Instead, he tried to teach me about my knees. He told me that there were certain activities that aggravated the condition: roller-skating, running, tennis. *Things I loved to do.* And there were other activities that would strengthen the ligaments around my knees: bicycling, swimming.

Things I did not know how to do. He prescribed physical therapy where I would learn exercises that would strengthen the muscles that my legs don't naturally develop.

I went to physical therapy, but I refused to stop skating and running. In fact, I wrapped my knees in braces and ACE bandages just so I could run track in high school. I preferred the pain of the dislocation to learning new sports.

I can barely believe how stubborn I was. I think part of that was determination. I didn't think my knee condition should stop me from doing the things that brought me joy. I think the other part was attitude. I didn't think of myself as having "bad knees." I just thought that they were different. "Different" meant that I would have to make a couple adjustments. After all, they were the only knees I'd ever known.

At a family reunion years later, I saw a great uncle moving his kneecaps around his knee the way I could. The younger children sat around amazed. I tugged my mother's shirt and said, "See, like ME!"

The older I got, the more sensitive my knees became. Running became too painful. The roller-rink became a mere memory from the '80s. A particular dislocating episode sent me to a physical therapist who told me that I had to learn how to walk again. She watched my kneecaps move side to side, above and out of the groove in which they should lie, and said, "You can't keep walking like that."

Wish someone had told me that when I was eight. At twenty-something, it was pretty difficult to learn a new way to do something so ordinary. She also showed me how to tape my knees into place while I was relearning my daily activity.

The crutches are for more severe incidents. When my kneecap dislocates and causes great pain, I use the crutches. I rest and apply ice and elevate and wrap my knee in bandages. My kneecap moves back into place, but the pain and weakness can last for weeks. Once the pain lasted for three months.

At first, I was grateful for the crutches that took the pressure off my aching leg. Before long, I was pouty! I wanted to dance and wear heels and go to the gym. There I would be—in the gym, with bandages and crutches, trying to lift weights. My new orthopedic surgeon forbade it. He said, "After it stops hurting, use the crutches for *another* month. You have to rest in order to heal."

It took me years to understand my depressive condition in the same way I understand my knees. I saw the association in a series of questions:

- Perhaps, there's nothing wrong with me? Maybe I'm just different. (After all, this is the only me that I've got.)
- Perhaps there are other people in my family who can relate to what I'm experiencing?
- What if I avoided the people and activities and practices that aggravate my condition?
- What if I did things that made me strong?
- Even if it doesn't happen naturally?
- Can I learn something new that will help me?
- What if I committed to something new, even if it's so basic that I feel as if I'm starting over again as a child?
- Maybe a therapist can give me something that can hold me together while I'm learning?

This curious comparison led me to three conclusions that have been important for me:

1. A depressive condition will not stop me from doing things that I enjoy.
2. It's not about a cure but about making adjustments.

3. Medication is not a sign of weakness. It's a crutch that will let me rest so I can heal.

These realizations changed both my life and my faith. With my knees, it was easy to forget how much faith I engaged. I trusted the crutches to hold me up when I wasn't strong enough to do it for myself. This kind of faith feels much harder with a mental health challenge. I need to trust various practices and medications and people. I need to trust that they will support me when I feel weak.

This is the opposite of a lot of what I've been taught about fortitude and faith:

- You have to believe for yourself.
- You can't get by on your mama's salvation.
- If you want it done right, you have to do it yourself.

This solo-mission, Energizer-Bunny stuff was not Jesus' way. Jesus often retreated from ministry and crowds to rest. In the last, most difficult days of his life, holy texts remind us that Jesus needed support. He asked his friends to sit with him and pray through a torturous night (Matthew 26:36-44). One friend carried the cross for him when he was tired (Mark 15:21-22). Another person offered vinegar while he hung on the cross (Matthew 27:48).

Rest. Help. Community. Support. Crutch.

What would it mean to think of Jesus with crutches? Does that make him weak?

For some people, a crutch is an excuse not to walk on one's own. Because of my knees, I know that crutches are the exact opposite. They are the instruments that allow me to function in the world.

We all need to rest sometimes.

We all need undergirding.

It's really the only way to heal.

~

Exploration
Do you have crutches? How do you rest when you need to heal?

Reflection
What can help undergird you when
you need something to lean on?

deeper than memory

My Jewish friends have a mezuzah on the right side of the door-frames of their homes. The mezuzah indicates that this is a Jewish home and that the inhabitants are protected, whether they are inside the home or outside of it. This small container on the doorpost contains passages from the Sh'ma or V'ahavta, the central affirmation of Jewish faith. Mezuzot contain parchment inside the container with the words from Deuteronomy 6:4-9 and Deuteronomy 11:13-21. On the outside of many mezuzah is the word *Shaddai*, a name for G-d.

While the posting of a mezuzah is a uniquely Jewish tradition, I think other people can learn from the practice. The mezuzah silently signifies identity to the outside world. It reaffirms the core teachings of faith. It calls us to remember. The first passage of the text contained in the mezuzah reads:

> Hear, O Israel: The Lord our God is one Lord: and thou shalt love the Lord thy God with all thine heart, and with all thy soul, and with all thy might. And these words, which I command thee this day, shall be in thine heart: and thou shalt teach them diligently

unto thy children, and shalt talk of them when thou sittest in thine house, and when thou walkest by the way, and when thou liest down, and when thou risest up. And thou shalt bind them for a sign upon thine hand, and they shall be as frontlets between thine eyes. And thou shalt write them upon the posts of thy house, and on thy gates.

While there are many messages contained in this passage, I am attracted most by the edict to remember. The Sh'ma reminds us to approach God with love. The scripture reminds us that our relationship with God is not just words but something we should keep in our hearts. The verse reminds us to remember our faith. I hear the commandments to teach and talk about and write about and walk about faith as a reminder that our faith should permeate all parts of our lives. Our faith is not something we express only on holy days. Rather, our faith should become a part of who we are.

Memory is a central theme in this section of Deuteronomy. In the chapters following this passage, God reminds the ancient Israelites that they must remember their relationship with God. The mezuzah is one of several concrete things that the ancient Israelites (and contemporary Jewish people) are asked to do to remember God. There appears to be a strong connection between rituals and holding God in our hearts.

This speaks strongly to me as someone who lives with a depressive condition. On the one hand, memory is not to be trusted. Depression can bend and twist my mind so that I can only remember what is bad. I remember all the griefs and pains of my life. I remember them with full force. When I am depressed, I cannot remember what it feels like to feel good. My only access to happiness is as dim as watching a slide show of someone else's childhood activities.

In those moments, I cannot trust my memory. I cannot remember joy. I cannot remember love. I cannot feel the goodness of God. I have to search for something deeper than memory.

And yet it is when my own sense of history is least reliable that I need to remember who I am, even when—especially when—I can't feel it.

So I write it down. I write down the things that I can't remember. For years, I kept a folded note card in my wallet with a couple sentences about who I am. It had things on it like this:

- I am a teacher.
- I am a minister.
- I am a friend.
- I am loved by many.
- I am living my grandparents' dreams.
- I am called by God.

When I found myself having bouts of anxiety, I'd slip into a restroom or corner and pull out my card and read it to myself. Some nights, I read it before going to bed, stuffing the card under the pillow as I fell asleep. The card was my personal doorpost. It was the place where I wrote down the things I believed. Until I could hold them in my heart, I read them off this card.

There are many psychological and spiritual traditions that recommend affirmations. Some individuals and communities use affirmations to maintain a positive outlook on self and the world. Others believe that the connection between our beliefs and our experiences is so close that affirmations can change what occurs in the world around us. At their best, affirmations help us live into being our highest selves.

Although they sound like affirmations, I've rarely thought of the words on my card in that way. These sentences were my lifelines. They were the things I held onto when I couldn't trust my mind, my heart, or my powers of recall. These words helped me connect to my deepest self. They got me to the one thing that was deeper than the power of memory.

Some people call this faith. Other people call it truth. Some people call it ritual.

For me, the note card became the indication of my humanity. It reminded me of my connection to people and beings greater than myself. It kept me on the safe side of a dangerous abyss. It helped me to love myself. These are the things I think God wants me to know—not just in depressions, but in every part of who I am.

~

Exploration
What do you think God wants you to remember about yourself?

Reflection
What six things would you write on a card?

waiting

When I first finished divinity school, I subscribed to a journal of Christian spirituality called *Weavings*. That was when I first heard of the concept of "active waiting." Often associated with the liturgical seasons of Lent and Advent, "active waiting" describes the way in which believers wait for a great spiritual event. In the Christian tradition, this spiritual event is often associated with Jesus: waiting for Jesus' birth; waiting for the second coming of Christ; waiting for the crucifixion and resurrection; waiting for Jesus to be revealed; waiting for the Holy Spirit to come.

In the days and weeks after the crucifixion and resurrection of Jesus, the disciples are often portrayed as waiting. I am fascinated by Luke's way of recounting this. The disciples have interacted with a risen Jesus. They have broken bread with him. They are talking amongst each other. Jesus appears again, speaks some words of wisdom, and concludes with these words: "And see I am sending upon you what God promised; so stay here in the city until you have been clothed with power from on high" (Luke 24:49). Then Jesus walks awhile with the disciples and, as the tradition names it, ascends into heaven.

While there is rich theological material to explore about whether or not Jesus ascended into heaven, whether the resurrection is heavenly or earthly, and whether the resurrection is bodily or metaphorical, what really captures my attention is the way the disciples are told to wait.

> *Stay here*
> *Stay here until*
> *Stay here until the power comes*
> *Wait*
> *Just wait*

So they wait. They go to the city and wait. But, the scripture goes on to say, the disciples don't sit around twiddling their thumbs. Rather, they go to the temple and worship and praise God continually. They wait actively.

The great priest and author Henri Nouwen says that waiting in scripture is not like waiting for a late bus. He writes:

> Those who are waiting are waiting very actively. They know that what they are waiting for is growing from the ground on which they are standing. . . . That's the secret. The secret of waiting is the faith that the seed has been planted, that something has begun. Active waiting means to be present fully to the moment in the conviction that something is happening where you are and that you want to be present to it. . . . Waiting, then, is not passive.

Spiritual leaders often use this concept of active waiting to help us to develop the spiritual art of patience. We should practice waiting with prayer and worship and spiritual disciplines. Because, they say, we trust that Jesus will be born, that the Holy Spirit will come, that Christ will return. The liturgical seasons of Lent and Advent remind us to ritually practice waiting for God and trusting in God's promises.

Contemporary society is often accused of being bad at waiting. We're impatient. We've become accustomed to a greater level of immediate gratification than previous generations. Technology facilitates this. We are able to search online information we want. We have twenty-four-hour news cycles. Media images flash by quickly. We don't have to wait in the ways that previous generations waited. We're not even accustomed to waiting.

There's a lot of waiting that occurs in the lives of people who live with depression. In between the desire to be well and wellness is a lot of waiting. We wait to feel better. We wait to get better.

One of the worst periods of waiting is the season when one waits for medication to work. Psychiatrists will often say that it takes about six weeks to begin to feel the effects of psychotropic medications. And so we have to be patient. We can't expect to feel better immediately.

This is a tortuous kind of waiting. After all the time of desperate illness, after finally deciding to be well, after finding a doctor you can afford and get to, who seems to understand what you're going through, you're given medication and told that it should start to kick in, say, six weeks or so. Could anything be crueler?

In my life, this kind of waiting has an active component as well. Waiting for medication to work is figuring out how strong to steep ginger in tea to cut the incessant nausea of the new pills. Waiting is lying very still on the couch because walking from one room to another in my small apartment makes me dizzy. Waiting is making bland foods with lots of nutrition because I vomit everything spicy and tasty for two weeks. Waiting is driving on curbs and parking at an angle for weeks until I realize that the medication affected my vision and that was somewhere in the two pages of fine print I received from the pharmacist. Waiting is taking the other pill to get rid of the anxiety caused by the pill that is supposed to make me happy. Waiting is calling the doctor back after declaring I can take it no more, and picking another drug, and going to the pharmacist and trying it all over again.

This is the unseen active waiting for many people who live with mental health challenges. Waiting for health. Waiting for happiness. Waiting for the holy spirit of wellness. Waiting for a change to come.

Sometimes I wonder if the Christian tradition hasn't sanitized the disciples' active waiting. I wonder if the Gospel writers made the disciples more patient and pious because the writers knew the end of the story. After all, when the early Christians find themselves waiting for the second coming of Jesus far longer than they expected, we get more stories of impatience and frustration. I wonder if the disciples weren't as anxious and scared and tired as depressed folk can be when waiting for medication to work. I wonder if our religious faith might not feel more accessible if we told that story.

I'm not suggesting that we shouldn't try to cultivate patience or that spiritual practices are to be eschewed. Prayer and worship are good things. But today, I'm not willing to glorify waiting either. Sometimes waiting sucks. Sometimes waiting feels horrible. Sometimes waiting seems like a harsh penalty meted out to someone who has finally admitted what's wrong and finally found a doctor.

This may be a truism of faith: that there's a lot of painful waiting involved. This may also be the only short cut to waiting for medication to work: faith. I've never heard a doctor say it this way, but they're asking you to have faith in the pill. Have faith that it will work eventually. Have faith that if this one doesn't work, then they will find another one that will. Have faith in the process of feeling crappy before you feel better.

~

Exploration
What do you do when you're waiting?

Reflection
How can you have faith while waiting?

evidence

I find comfort in those two tones that indicate an episode of a *Law and Order* franchise is coming on. I don't mind watching reruns because I've usually forgotten the outcome. I feel the same way about the *CSI* franchises and the show *House*. This might be my personal television vice, but I suspect that it's part of a wider fascination with evidence. That is, many people have become increasingly interested in various forms of evidence—through technology, skepticism, a need for healing, or a quest for justice—and how it plays out around us.

These television shows affirm some of my beliefs about the world: I love that we always leave evidence of our presence in the world. I'm interested in what evidence counts—and what evidence is left out—when decisions get made. I realize that it often takes a team of people to figure out what's going on.

I thirst for evidence. This desire for proof can also be found in faith communities. Christian scriptures often portray Jesus' disciples as asking him for a sign. There's one example in John 6:30.

> So the disciples said to Jesus, "What sign are you going to give us then, so that we may see it and believe you? What work are you performing?"

This suggests to me that even when people have committed themselves to a cause or teaching or community, they still want proof that they're on the right track. In this case, the disciples want proof of God's presence.

Theologians and philosophers of religion have filled volumes talking about proofs for the existence of God. Thinkers from Anselm of Canterbury to Immanuel Kant argue that we know God exists because of what we see in the world—from creation to a sense of human morality. Of course, it must be remembered that these philosophers of religion and theologians are referring to a particular Christian God with certain attributes.

Likewise, religious scholars have also written extensively about religious experience. In this category, we ask: How do I know God is present? How do I know that God is with me?

In *The Varieties of Religious Experiences*, William James interviews a number of devout Christians and concludes that people themselves know when they have experienced God. The evidence of God that people give ranges from charismatic expressions to internal senses of peace and love.

Some communities demand more objective data. That is, other people should be able to confirm that God is present. Some insist that the ability to handle snakes or speak in tongues is necessary proof of the indwelling of God. Others find power in rituals like baptism and Eucharist. Still others argue that God's presence should be manifest in good works and moral behavior.

The same questions can be asked in the context of depressive conditions. How do I know? What is my evidence?

Therapeutic communities are very good at gathering evidence. If I understand the DSM (*Diagnostic and Statistical Manual of Mental Disorders*) model correctly, many mental health conditions are determined by aggregating symptoms. Clinicians look at the evidence before them and use this data to assess, treat, and hopefully heal. There are checklists and markers and questions. They seem to be asking the question: How do we know when something is wrong?

In the midst of this accumulation of information, there's something people rarely ask me when it comes to depressive conditions:

How do you know you are well?

Is it an internal feeling? New behaviors? Or does one simply fail to show the symptoms that declared one's condition in the first place?

Here I learn from the faithful. Faith communities do not ask for proof of God's absence. They inquire about affirmation of God's presence. This questioning reminds me that wellness is more than the absence of negative symptoms. Wellness is something positive. Wellness can actually be normal.

How do you know you are well? For me, it's small things.

- Everyday activities are everyday (not monumental feats).
- Breakfast tastes good.
- I laugh.

I need bits of evidence that I can piece together. Although my faith persists when I feel horrible, I'm more like the disciples than I want to admit. I need signs and wonders that I'm on the right path.

In a world that's often more interested in what's wrong, I find power in the evidence, however small it may be, that things are good.

Exploration
How do you define wellness for yourself?

Reflection
What is your evidence of wellness?

not at war

"Sticks and stones may break my bones, but I'll never forget what you said."

That's the truer version of the playground retort bullied children are supposed to use when maliciously teased. Although the original—"sticks and stones may break my bones, but words will never hurt me"—can be quickly rolled off the tongue, many of us do remember and internalize the harsh words we hear from those around us.

The words we use for ourselves, the words we use for each other, the way we name ourselves, the boxes we put people in, the way we name God: it all matters.

Words matter because our words reveal our values. They reveal how we really feel about the world around us, and what and who we aspire to be.

That's why Mary Daly wrote, "If God is male, then the male is God."

This is why one says "people who live with disabilities" rather than "handicapped people."

The way we talk and write and name ourselves and those around us says something about the narrowness or the complexity of love and life.

I appreciate the way liberationists have paid attention to language. I like the way feminists, poets, and health advocates (to name a few) remind us about the power of our words.

This becomes particularly relevant to me as one who lives with a depressive condition and as one who is not a fan of war and the military industrial complex.

In 1999, my friend and fellow Vanderbilt University Divinity School graduate Carol Orsborn cowrote a book about her experience with breast cancer. Carol and three other women who had been diagnosed with breast cancer riled against the way that the medical industry and wider society referred to living with breast cancer in the metaphorical language of war. Carol, Linda Quigley, Karen Stroup, and Susan Kuner wrote about this in their book, *Speak the Language of Healing: Living with Breast Cancer without Going to War.*

Former surgeon general of the United States Jocelyn Elders said this about their book:

> These four women . . . faced the terrifying diagnosis
> of breast cancer and courageously refused to go to war
> against their own bodies. For them, the disease was
> not an enemy to be vanquished but a part of them-
> selves to explore, understand and accept.

I like how Jocelyn Elders summarizes Carol and her friends:

refusing to go to war against their own bodies

This resonates with me and my faithful living with a depressive condition. It's easy for me to be frustrated and downright mad at the force within me that triggers so easily with stress, weather, and the vicissitudes of life. It's easy to think of battling depression. The medication, therapy, exercise, meditation, and numerous other techniques become part of my healthy warrior arsenal that will "conquer" or "survive" depression.

I remember the day my therapist asked me to stop thinking of depression as an enemy. I cut my eyes at her and scowled. *Are you joking? Something inside of me can take me out, and I'm not supposed to fight it?*

Author and teacher Parker J. Palmer writes of this cogently in his book *Let Your Life Speak*. He recalls a therapist saying, "You seem to look upon depression as the hand of an enemy trying to crush you. . . . Do you think you could see it instead as the hand of a friend pressing you down to ground on which it is safe to stand?"

"Friend"? Could a depressive condition be a friend? Could it be a part of myself to explore, understand, and accept?

It's taken me years to stretch my original understanding of depression to one that refuses to go to war against my own body.

Like my friend Carol and her coauthors, I find myself in a minority position. The overwhelming majority of our Western culture and society prefers the larger, more powerful, and more monied world that linguistically supports the images of war and destruction. As a result, I find myself having to renew my commitment to peaceful, healing language again and again.

This came to me recently in yoga class.

I went to yoga because I needed something to help me feel better. I was pulling out the yoga tool from my sheath of stay-healthy warrior implements. Of course, yoga doesn't make me feel like a survivor. Instead, I am reminded of all the ways I need to improve my balance and muscle strength. I always fall in a heap on the floor trying some pose I think I can do.

But doing yoga reminds me of key insights to live by:

- Breathe.
- Stretch.
- Balance.

These aren't ammunition to wrestle and subdue what is within me. These reminders are ways of slowing down and connecting with what is inside of me. These become principles that help me heal rather than fight.

I'm glad that there is at least one religious tradition—in this case, Hinduism—willing to share its practices with those of us outside that tradition, a tradition that emphasizes the connection between the body, soul, and purpose.

While Christian traditions have spiritual disciplines and practices, my religious upbringing inherited the most dualistic, body-depriving aspects of Christianity. I have to look much harder at the Bible and Christian history to find remnants of body-affirming practices.

When I take time to breathe, stretch, and balance, I become stronger. Not only does my body become stronger, but I become stronger in life with a depressive condition.

When I feel strong, I save the clinical diagnosis for clinicians who use it as shorthand to guide them in helping me be healthy. I don't think of myself as ill or disordered, as the dominant language in the field might indicate. I think of myself as "Monica" who lives with a "condition."

When I feel strong, I reserve the word "crazy" for my own unrealistic expectations that need to be discarded. I don't use it to refer to myself, my friends, or even strangers.

I'm not calling depression my friend.

I usually just salute the sun every morning.

But these are very small steps as I refuse to go to war against myself.

~

Reflection
Do you find yourself using language of war
to speak about your condition?

Reflection
What language can help you heal —rather than fight?

learning to swim

I recently learned how to swim. I decided it was time to learn. I asked friends for a swim instructor referral, looked it up, and enrolled in a class. A week later, I was swimming across the pool. It was that easy. In my own defense, I knew what to do. I just wasn't very good at doing it. It's not just me. It's a big catch-22 for adults who can't swim: You're afraid of the water because you can't swim. And you can't swim because you're afraid of the water. Ultimately, you have to trust the teacher and jump in the water.

As I've been proudly sharing the fact that I now know how to swim, my friends have raised several questions. These questions can be summarized into two larger queries:

1. So you can swim laps now?

No. Are you joking?! I just learned how to swim. I still have to practice several times a week. I have to get in the water again. Over and over again. And I have to keep remembering how to kick my legs, move my arms, turn my head, and breathe. It's not that easy. I assume it will get easier the more I do it. I predict that, after awhile, I may not even have to think that hard about technique. I can just enjoy the exercise.

The second question is actually more profound:

2. How did you get so old without learning how to swim?

Here's the not-so-subtle subtext: What were you doing as a kid? Isn't it some kind of parental responsibility to make sure kids know how to swim?

It's a fair question. My parents enrolled me in kiddie swim classes. They sent me to the YMCA and other summer programs with my cousins. My cousins learned. I did not. Honestly, I wasn't motivated. I wasn't excited about water. And I was content to splash around in the shallow end. My everyday life was not diminished by my inability to swim.

I learned to swim when I decided I wanted to learn. And once I decided, it wasn't difficult, but I wasn't going to become proficient in a week, either. That's what it's like when one explores something new.

I'm coming to realize that living with a mental health challenge is a constant encounter with "the new." Every so often, I have to try new things. Doctors will often reiterate this when prescribing psychotropic medication. It's new. *Your body has to get used to it. It might not kick in immediately. It affects every person differently. You may have to try more than one medication.* Several years ago, the medication I was taking stopped working. Apparently that happens. And there I was, back on the "new train."

In some ways, finding medication is easier than the other new things one must encounter with a mental health challenge. Finding the right medication is truly an experience of trial and error. It's not fun, but one also has little agency. Most of "the new" is about new skills, new patterns, and new ways of operating in the world. And we have to do something.

Since my acceptance of my own condition, "the new" has included getting regular exercise, eating foods with particular nutrients, getting adequate sleep, doing research, learning healthy ways of dealing with stress, reducing life stressors in the first place, finding doctors I trust, talking to friends I trust, meeting other people who live with the same condition as me—the list goes on.

Yes, all this was new for me. Before, I was fairly intermittent about my exercise, ate the foods I liked, chose work over sleep, and used default methods of coping to reduce the existential pain I was feeling. And, for the record, I was happy to keep most of this to myself.

But I wanted to live. For me, that was the motivation I needed to trust my instructor/therapist and jump in the waters of life. And then I had to keep at it. I have to keep doing the things I know are healthy—even when I'm tired, frustrated, have a bad experience with a doctor or medication, or meet people who don't understand me or who judge me.

It's another catch-22: I'm afraid of doing new things; it's hard. But things won't get easier or better if I don't do something new.

I'm encouraged by how Jesus talks about the importance of doing something new. One day the disciples ask Jesus why they practice their spirituality differently from the Pharisees (Matthew 9:14-17). Jesus answers with three metaphors. One of them mentions that we must put new wine in new bottles, or else the bottles will break. This is how I hear Jesus:

If we want to experience something new,
we have to do something new.

I believe that each day can bring something new. Sometimes it's an occasion to celebrate that I'm learning and doing well. Other times it's another opportunity to practice something I'm still learning. If swimming is an apt analogy, I predict that after awhile, the "new" will become second nature, and I can just enjoy the process.

~

Exploration
What new experience do you want?

Reflection
What new thing will you have to do? How can you practice?

sacrament

"You have to believe in it. It won't work if you don't have some faith that it will work."

These are the words my friend said to me years ago when I realized I could no longer manage my depressive condition without medication. Friend to friend, depressive to depressive, minister to minister: he told me to have faith.

I knew how to have faith in God. We prayed and preached about that for a living. I was not used to having faith in a pill.

I'm the kind of person who has to have a raging headache for at least six hours before I'll take a painkiller. I've been misdiagnosed more than once, given the wrong medication, and suffered through weeks of vomiting and head-to-toe rashes. And that was for medical conditions far less complicated than the human brain. By the time of this conversation, I had negative faith in medicine and its competency when it came to my body. In my worst medication-related reactions, I lay down in bed and declared I would rather die right here before I went back to *that doctor* again.

But I didn't want to die, and when death at my own hands became a closer reality than I could stand, I called the psychiatrist. In the days before the appointment, my friend reminded me I was going to have to muster up some faith in more than God if I wanted to get better.

At the time, I lacked the ability to see how my friend was connecting my attitude and my health. I knew that some religious traditions believe that you can heal illnesses through prayer and meditation. I knew that some traditions disallow procedures that some medical doctors consider life-saving, like blood transfusions. I had read about these religious trajectories. I didn't know anyone who lived them, and I was not a part of these traditions. My Christian faith had never taught me to eschew allopathic medicine.

But lay and medical personnel alike are aware of what many religions have long taught: your mental and spiritual approach to your body and healing make a difference in how you heal.

And who's to say God doesn't work in and through medication?

"You have faith in inanimate things all the time," my friend continued.

I had faith in a chair—that it wouldn't collapse when I sat on it.

"Try to believe in the medication. Believe that it will help you."

I decided to believe, but more through a combination of desperation and trust in my friend than because of spiritual maturity.

The twice-daily pill swallowing served as a kind of Eucharist or holy meal where I trusted in the mystery that what I put in my mouth would connect me to God, myself, and others.

What I could not have imagined then was how much faith it takes to get *off* medication.

There is a common idea that a diagnosis of a mental health challenge means starting psychotropic medication and staying on it for the rest of one's life. That's what the nurse at the HMO told me. This is true for some people.

But there are also many reasons why people who live with depressive conditions stop taking medication. Here are a few examples:

- It's contraindicated with another medication that must be taken for a more serious or pressing condition.
- It threatens the health of a growing fetus (if you're a woman planning to birth children).
- Another medication might work better, but your system has to be med-free to start something new.
- The medication is for one pole of a bipolar depression but unhelpful when moving toward the other pole.

These are just a few of the reasons I've heard from my doctors and friends who live with depressive conditions. I've gone off medication for some of the reasons listed here.

If going on medication requires the patience of a saint, getting off medication requires the faith of one.

First there are the side effects. Mine have included nausea, insomnia, unbelievable sleepiness, and headaches. Not just for hours, but for days and weeks. I've literally taken to bed and wished for a detox center.

I've marveled at the power of the medication—to stabilize me, treat threatening symptoms, and then undo my stability.

What is so wrong with my brain that no longer taking a couple of pills throws my whole body off kilter?

And then there's life without it. I needed so much faith to take the pills—the faith I mustered to believe what I'm not: I'm not less of a human being or less than God's beloved creation; I'm not a wimp who couldn't handle life, nor am I a believer whose piety failed her. All that faith means nothing when the meds are gone.

Without meds, I am wholly dependent on a new trinity of regular sleep, exercise, and disciplined healthy eating. These are not optional. They are the practices I need to be okay and, if I'm lucky, well and happy.

Oh, and there's the anger and resentment. I am completely convinced that other people, normal people, don't have to do all this. I know it's a lie that depression tells me. But I still believe it. I don't want to add one more item to the daily to-dos: tell the depression liar that there are no "normal people" and everyone should be doing these things.

I suspect that my Protestant heritage makes this kind of faith more difficult for me. As Martin Luther and his many successors critiqued the abuses of the Catholic Church of their day, they stressed the importance of biblical text and of faith as belief. They wanted to make God and religion more accessible to ordinary people.

This Christian trajectory often loses a more sacramental understanding of faith. Catholics and Orthodox Christians did a far better job of reminding people that God is in the elements and the rituals. Engaging in these things was also an experience of God.

- Is it God when my alarm goes off indicating that it's time for me to go to the gym?
- Is it a divine calling to have my head on the pillow no later than 10:30 every night?
- Is organic tropical fruit holier than my constant chocolate craving?

In my world of living with a depressive condition—with and without meds—the answer to these questions is yes. It means trusting that there is some salvation in the elements and the rituals.

∼

Exploration
What is one ordinary thing in your life in which
you need to remember God's presence?

Reflection
What rituals can help your faith?

Embracing
Death as a
New Beginning

peace and comfort

I like the way the Gospel of John talks about the Holy Spirit. In Jesus' farewell to his disciples (John 14–17), he talks about a Spirit—a Comforter—that will come to bring peace to the disciples after his death. I like how Jesus knows that his departure will be disruptive. I like Jesus' acknowledgment that death leaves us reeling.

John 14:27 recalls Jesus' words in this way:

> *Peace* I leave with you; my peace I give to you. I do not give to you as the world gives. Do not let your hearts be troubled, and do not let them be afraid.

As a minister, I memorize these words and repeat them at funerals and memorial services. These words are supposed to reassure the grieving. I most appreciate the recognition of how death and loss really feel. Death and loss turn our lives upside down. Death and loss make it hard to put one foot in front of the other. Death and loss keep us up at night and steal our appetites. Or drive us to all sorts of places seeking rest and comfort. Indeed, peace is elusive when unwelcome death is nigh.

I value most how death is not the end of Jesus' story with the disciples. I'm not referring to a resurrection. I'm referring to Spirit. Jesus suggests that once he is gone, a Holy Spirit will replace him. He may die, but a Spirit lives on. He will become an ancestor.

I admit that I did not understand this by reading the Bible. I understood this when I heard Sweet Honey in the Rock's song "Breaths" based on the poem "Les Souffles" (often translated "Invocation of the Dead") by twentieth-century Senegalese poet Birago Diop. Sweet Honey sings:

> 'Tis the ancestors' breath when the fire's voice is heard
> 'Tis the ancestors' breath in the voice of the waters
> They are in the rustling trees, they are in the groaning woods
> They are in the crying grass, they are in the moaning rocks
> The dead are not under the earth
> Those who have died have never never left
> The dead have a pact with the living

Many African Christian theologians have referred to Jesus as an ancestor. Charles Nyamiti talks about this in *Christ as Our Ancestor*, and Emmanuel Martey refers to it in *African Theology: Inculturation and Liberation*. It's not a perfect comparison. For many African cultures, the term "ancestor" requires a gentler death than Jesus experienced, living offspring, and a familial connection. But Jesus' life had a lasting impact, and, in his physical absence, he protects, guards, and guides us. This, many African theologians have insisted, makes Jesus like an ancestor.

When I read the Gospels from the disciples' perspective, Spirit is the ancestor. Jesus leaves. Jesus dies, Jesus returns, Jesus tells the disciples to wait, and then he leaves again. Jesus is gone. But the Spirit comes. And knowing that death leaves us distraught, the Spirit comes granting peace and comfort and help.

I've often found this much more biblical than true. When death comes, I don't feel peace. When I realize that parts of me have died in the depths of depression, I'm not very comforted. I'm downright inconsolable. And being told to *wait* for peace and power and hope—like in Luke's description of the ascension—is not exactly inspiring.

But it is a way forward. Jesus tells us that there is not just life after death, but there is peace, comfort, and help. When we die, we still live on.

In some ways I know this. I come from people who light candles, interpret dreams, and visit gravesites. We've always assumed that the spirits of those who have died are close to us.

This is why I like Pentecost so much: ancestral spirits are more common than resurrections.

It took me much longer to apply this idea to myself. Acknowledging that parts of me die in each depression is a first step. Giving myself permission to mourn is a second step. Part of that mourning is waiting—almost begging—for peace and comfort.

These scriptures remind me that although I've lost something big, it's not completely gone. The part of me that died—well, it became an ancestor too. It's not an active part of me—not even if I want it to be—but it hasn't left me. It still has my memories. It can still teach me. It can still guide me, even if it's not who I am anymore. I've heard some psychologists talk about one's inner child this way. I like to think that the parts of me that die—sometimes violently and loudly, other times quietly passing away in the night—don't just float away into some ether. I never abandon myself.

I'm not sure that this is what Jesus meant in those farewell discourses. It's definitely not how most Christians have read it. But there is something comforting in knowing that we don't hang ourselves out to dry. I find a door opens on the path to peace when I don't have to completely let go of my past. I like knowing that I can be a Spirit to myself.

So I find these words to be holy:

> *Those who have died have never never left*
> *The dead have a pact with the living*

~

Exploration
What parts of your past are important to you?

Reflection
How can you keep them alive?

needing the past

My father was a student of history and ensured that I would be as well. More specifically, he was a student of African American history. I knew who Mary McLeod Bethune and George Washington Carver were before I went to first grade. I read Carter G. Woodson's *The Miseducation of the Negro* in the fourth or fifth grade. And I was familiar with the writings of African American historians in high school.

For my father, this was greater than the adage "If you don't know where you've been, you can't know where you are going." For him, knowing one's history, especially one's suppressed cultural history, is a part of being alive. It's part of what makes us whole.

It was easy for me to apply this same idea to my personal past. As a child, I loved to ask my mother stories about how things were when she was growing up. What games did she play? Who did she like? How did Grandma do her hair? I liked flipping through old pictures. I didn't just want to know her stories—I wanted to know the stories of the family. I wanted to know about my paternal grandmother's known slave ancestors and the blacksmith shop. I wanted to know about my orphaned maternal grandmother and how her family sharecropped cotton. I wanted to know who raised them when their parents died and how he was related to us. I wanted to know why so many of my cousins have derivatives of the same family names.

My mother told me most of what I wanted to know, even when my grandparents were alive. My grandparents didn't like to talk about the past. They said it was too painful.

I now understand that their histories of death, poverty, racism, migration, and loss were not so atypical of other Native Americans and African Americans of their social and geographical background. I also understand that talking about the past might have felt like reliving something that they worked hard to transcend.

I've never thought of myself as someone who clings to the past. I think about my future. I set goals. Yet in my ongoing depressions, there are few things I want more than to go back in time—even though I don't say it that way. I say things like:

I want my life back.
I want things to be like they were before X happened.

I want to go back in time. When I put it that way, I know it's not possible. I know I cannot do anything over. I know I cannot be who I was. That simple realization can feel crushing when I can't envision new things I will do and when I don't know how I will grow. I generally know that I will go on. Tomorrow will come and bring new activities. There are still goals to attain. And I will evolve into a new—and hopefully more mature—version of myself. Often I can't see the path to that place. In deep depressions I don't even trust that such a place even exists.

In the space amidst the knowledge that I can't go back in time, my inability to see in front of myself, and my desperate need for peace, I need the past. I need the good parts of the past. I need to remember that the last depressive episode didn't kill me. I need to remember that I have been happy before. I need to remember the faith that I can't feel at that moment. I need the past to come to me.

I believe the past comes to those of us in the present. In the simplest form, the past comes to me in my memory. Even when it's difficult, I *can* remember.

Sometimes this is a mystical belief that the spirits of my deceased relatives are still with me. It can be as ordinary as thinking that my grandmother would be proud of me on those special occasions when I wish she were there. Or it can be as complicated as Freudian analyses of the dreams I still have about her.

In the traditional religion of the Yoruba people of southwest Nigeria, cultural ancestors (known as the orisha) come to the community in individuals who dance and sing and drum. Anthropologists have called this "spirit possession."

With popular images of spirit possession like the movie *The Exorcist* engraved in Western consciousness, it's hard to think of "spirit possession" as a good thing. But religion reminds me that it can be. It can be one way the past comes to me in the present— since I can't go back into the past.

Some Christians experience the Holy Spirit this way. For people in charismatic traditions, it can manifest as "speaking in tongues" and "holy dancing." For most, the Holy Spirit is a way of naming the fact that even though Jesus is no longer walking on the earth, his message and divine presence live on.

These faith traditions suggest that Spirit does not come just to remind me that the past once existed. They suggest that Spirit comes to remind me of the past in order to help me move into the future. For some people, this next move involves words of wisdom that can indicate which path to choose. For others, the move into the future involves sharing one's faith and inviting others into community. I understand it this way:

Through spirit, the past can teach and motivate the present.

In this sense my father was right. The past is part of what keeps us alive. And if I can't go back into the past, then I need the past to come to me. In my saddest, emptiest moments, I need memory and more. I need help. I need my ancestors—cultural and familial—to help me. I need spirit.

Because when death is near, learning and hoping can be a bridge toward life.

∽

Exploration
How do you connect to the best parts of your past?

Reflection
What motivates you most to keep going forward?

funerals for the living

I recently sat at dinner with a group of seminarians talking about whether or not theological education prepares student ministers for the everyday tasks of ministry. At this particular time, we spoke about how classes in liturgy prepare seminarians to conduct some of the key rituals of our trade: weddings and funerals. Weddings are fun, we all agreed. Funerals are quite difficult.

There's a part of planning funerals that isn't so complicated. Scriptures, sacred readings, hymns, obituary. Sitting with the grieving friends and family. The hard part is the eulogy. There's a lot of pressure to get the eulogy right. We're trained to talk with families and focus on the life of the individual. We're also supposed to provide hope: hope in God, hope that we will all meet on the other side (if that's what you believe), hope that life will go on. After all, the funerals are for the living, not for the one who has died.

One person recalled a funeral of a gang member. The eulogy was so inspiring that several members of the gang came down the aisle, dedicated their lives to God, and pledged to make changes for the better. Everyone at the table oohed and aahed. That's a good one. Most of us could not remember the eulogies we'd heard. Not even of close family members. Maybe the eulogies weren't that good. Maybe grief erased our memories.

Many people who write about depression describe it like grief. They say it's like a deep sadness. It's like heartbreak, agony, and despair all at once. I've never felt that way. I've always thought that grief was a walk in the park compared to depression. Grief has an identifiable cause. There are stages. It eases over time.

Depression has always felt like death to me. I'm not referring to suicide. I'm talking about what is lost. In every depressive episode, something is lost. Something dies. And it never returns. Sometimes it's the belief that you're not that sick. Sometimes it's a dream. Sometimes it's a concrete plan or goal. Sometimes it's a harmful lie you've told yourself or someone told you. Sometimes what dies needed to go. Other times, it seems you could have been perfectly fine without knowing this loss.

For many of us, this death is quiet and invisible. It's stealth. We may not know what was lost until we feel alive again. When we are able to whisper about what has happened, only our closest confidantes and therapists know what has died.

What if we had funerals to mark these kinds of deaths? After all, the ritual is there to honor that someone has died. The ritual is there for community to acknowledge that we should pause when there has been a great loss. The ritual is there to offer hope.

How would one structure this kind of funeral? Would there be scriptures, hymns, sacred readings? Who would attend? What do you say in the eulogy? Do you recall how wonderful the deceased was? Do you talk about how she made wonderful contributions to the world? Do you say our lives were the better for knowing her? Do you say it's okay to cry and scream over what and who has passed? Do you say that even when someone has died, there is still life after death? Do you say that even when something has died and it hurts like hell, something else is given the chance to live? Do you remind the living that they still have their memories? Do you tell the living—even the still-living person for whom something has died—that we will all meet on the other side, but we will be different? We will all be transformed by what death does to us.

I tried this once. When I realized that something very large inside of me died, I had a funeral. I had sacred readings and songs and dance. I wrote a eulogy. I invited friends who didn't completely understand what was going on. I went to Good Friday services. I did this for myself. Because I was the person living who needed hope in the face of the death of someone I loved.

I didn't know then that there was a template for this. There is a way to write an obituary for someone who has died but is still alive. I think this is what the Gospel writers tried to do. I like their approach. They talked about how Jesus was born, how they came to know him, what they liked best about him, what he did, whom he touched. They told their favorite stories about him. And, unlike most clergy in eulogies, they didn't shy away from talking about how he died. They realized that death was an important part of talking about new life.

∾

Exploration
Where do you find hope in the face of death?

Reflection
How can you honor a great loss in your life?

cry it out

I experience one of life's greatest pleasures when a child hugs me. Warm fuzzies head to toe in less than two seconds. When I was a child, hugging adults usually conveyed a familial or extended family relationship and joy for the adult's presence. And like many other children, there were occasions when I needed a hug so I could be calmed: when the wasp stung me, when leaving home, when my grandmother died.

I now understand how much the hug gives to an adult. Adults also receive a sense of dependence, fulfillment, comfort, and joy from the hugs. In hugs we absorb and diffuse pain, project and receive comfort, greet and celebrate, mourn and shudder. It's one of the few, quick-and-easy forms of mutuality in my life. Hugging creates empathy.

So I can understand how difficult it is when many parents and guardians go through the stage when they must let their child cry themselves to sleep. After days, weeks, and months of jumping at every cry, searching for the source of alarm, and learning the differences between a "hungry cry," a "tired cry," and the "I'm-scared-without-you cry," now, many experts say, "Let the child cry."

It goes against this basic maxim that Paul writes about in a letter to an early Christian community in Rome: "Rejoice with those who rejoice; weep with those who weep" (Romans 12:15).

Sometimes we need to be reminded to form community. Sometimes we need gentle prodding to remember that we are our brothers' and sisters' keepers. Sometimes a short scripture goads us into reaching out and hugging someone. Although we may need to hear these words repeated, it seems like an acceptable—even if ideal—rule by which to live in faith, family, and friendship.

The idea of letting a child cry himself to sleep can often grate against the empathy we've developed.

Those who advocate this practice refer to it as "self-soothing." One puts a child into her own bed or crib when she's awake and lets her soothe herself to sleep—without the rocking, cuddling, or cooing of the loving adult. The child often protests because it's a new experience, the constant comforter seems to be gone, and she hasn't yet developed the skill to calm herself. So the child cries and cries and cries. And the loving adults must quell the desire to run to the child. They need to let the child cry it out. They must trust that the need to sleep will compel the child to find a way to comfort herself. It's a way of helping children to mature.

I have found that this is not just a skill that tired babies must learn. It's a skill that I've had to learn and relearn myself. The angst of adolescence, the grief of missing deceased loved ones, and the chronic emotional pain of depression mean that I have cried myself to sleep on more occasions that I can count. Most of the time, this has come from necessity—not a desire to be mature and to comfort myself.

As a person living with a depressive condition, I have found anguish to be a frequent visitor. If I had it my way, I'd share it to dissipate its power, lean on the most dependable of friends, and have someone come in and rock me when I'm scared, I can't sleep, or something new seems daunting. Intellectually, I've known that's not possible. Emotionally, it's been a constant craving.

One therapist pointed this out to me when she said, "You have to learn to do for yourself what you are asking other people to do for you." I knew what she meant. I wanted other people to comfort me—to rock me and hold me and tell me that it's going to be okay. My therapist's point was simple, but it wasn't easy.

I had huge emotional expectations for some of the closest people in my life. That had to stop. I had to strip the codependent relationships from my life. *Don't call them at 2 am to talk me through the nightmare. Don't call them to come over and watch me sleep. Don't ask them to hold me together when I'm falling apart.* That was too much to ask. It wore people out. It was too much of a task for any one person to manage. And I would always be disappointed because no one can do that perfectly.

So I learned. I learned to curl up in a ball, wrap my arms around each other with my hands on my shoulders, and rock. I would imagine that someone—some Spirit, an imaginary friend, my mama, God—was rocking me. Someone was pulling the hair back from my eyes and rocking me and saying, "Shh, baby. It's going to be okay. Shh. It's going to be okay."

This became something I could invoke in the middle of the night—and there are always middle-of-the-night moments. I rocked myself to sleep. I cried it out. I soothed myself.

This worked for years and years. This was my silent personal way of living with some of the inexplicable, far-too-often nighttime pains of living with a depressive condition.

One difficult night, I invoked my normal routine. I had awakened from a dream in an anxiety attack. Even while sleeping, my mind was reviewing all the stressors in my life—magnifying them into insurmountable tasks. Short of breath, I started rocking. I curled into the fetal position and began speaking to myself. My "shhs" were probably audible. I invoked every breathing technique I had learned from yoga, chiropractic care, spiritual meditation, and respiratory integration. These are some of the practices that keep me well and calm in daylight hours. "Shh," I said between hyperventilating breaths.

It did not work. And in that moment, I knew what had died.

~

Exploration
When do you know that something has stopped working?

Reflection
How do you soothe yourself when you're anxious or scared?

falling

In 2001, the rock band Creed released their album *Weathered*, which featured a song that climbed into the top ten of the Billboard music charts. "One Last Breath" has stayed with me in the years since it received a lot of radio play because it so well describes how I can feel during a depressive episode.

My favorite verses say:

> *Please come now, I think I'm falling*
> *I'm holding to all I think is safe . . .*
> *But I'm down to one last breath, and with it let me say*
> *"Hold me now. I'm six feet from the edge and I'm thinking,*
> *Maybe six feet ain't so far down"*

This song came to me when I was talking with one of my best friends. I walked in circles in my small apartment kitchen as I held the phone to my ear.

"I can feel myself dying."

My friend was as alarmed as he should have been. As alarmed as I would have been if I had heard that sequence of words in the emotionless tone I was using.

I tried to explain. I often think of each depressive episode like a death. Something in me dies with each episode. Something new is reborn as well, but it often takes some time to notice it, to know what it was. To speak its name. And when we do, when we finally know that something has died and something has taken its place, we should ritualize it. We should hold a funeral or memorial service. We should throw a birthday party to cheer the new birth.

For me, this is the complete and public side of what really happens when faith traditions assert that God can do a new thing in us (Isaiah 43:19a). That when we live in faith and Spirit, we are new creations. Old things pass away and new things have come (2 Corinthians 5:17).

Sometimes I've lost a part of me that I had never chosen to lose—or at least not so painfully. Other times, I've shirked a childhood habit, a disillusion, or an unhealthy crutch. I acknowledge that even if good came from it, it did not feel good. And I acknowledge that wherever I am now is okay. Whoever I am now is loved by God and hence worthy of being loved and accepted by me.

Discerning these deaths and births is no easy feat. Sometimes a therapist guides me toward it. Other times I grapple for it on my own or stumble on it years after it has happened.

This is the kind of discerning that is best done in the new life. I reserve the human right *not* to seek the good or the lesson while I'm suffering. But sometime later—after the death, after the resurrection—then I can talk about it. The Gospel writers must have understood this well.

But in that moment, walking around my kitchen, I hit the realization too early. And I told my friend, "I feel myself dying. I don't know what is dying, but I feel like something is dying."

In the midst of balancing work and family and all the healthy things I'm supposed to do, I realized that I could not trust my mind. Alone with my thoughts, I was unlovable, unbearable, always right, terribly wrong, easily injured, completely misunderstood, and invisible. I waited the obligatory six weeks for the meds to kick in. I forbade myself from making any important emotional decisions until the fog cleared.

In this season, I felt myself dying. "But," I told my friend, "I don't know what I'm losing."

We checked in about doctors, work, meds, exercise. I affirmed that work and meds were all that I could do just then.

"I'm worried about you," he said.

"Me too."

There can be a fine line between feeling death and making it happen. Voicing it kept me on the nonsuicidal side of the line. Saying it aloud to someone who understood didn't make it stop. But it disarmed its power.

Talking to my friend, I was barely aware of that. I didn't know what was dying or how long I would feel it. I held onto the message of the resurrection that even though I felt I was dying, I wasn't.

I don't know every world religion. I barely know a couple well. But it seems to me that this is the core teaching of Christianity's resurrection, Buddhism's nirvana, Yoruba traditional religion's becoming an ancestor (to name a few).

Even when it seems like you're dying . . . you're not.

❧

Exploration
What disarms the power of death for you?

Reflection
How do you describe the feeling of loss and sadness in depression?

flight

Human beings have long admired and envied a bird's ability to soar through the skies. I imagine that this initiated the design of the kite and reached its pinnacle in space exploration. I do most of my flying on commercial airplanes as I travel from one end of the country to see family and friends or to give lectures and speeches.

Although American inventors Wilbur and Orville Wright are often credited with inventing the first airplane, they readily admitted to their inspirations. They learned from the attempts of other inventors: Otto Lilienthal, Octave Chanute, Sir George Cayley, and Samuel Langley. The Wright brothers could fly because they learned from previous successes and failures.

I appreciate this invention in part because I use it so much. I most appreciate my experience on planes for the lessons about getting into the heights of the sky:

- Buckle up.
- It takes time, power, a team of people, and a bit of noise to ascend.
- No matter how I rely on it, flight is still a fragile mystery.

These are the lessons I need to remember the most when I can feel myself falling. When I don't feel that I am in the air, but rather that I am sinking into the earth. When I know something is dying, I need to remember how to fly.

One night, I knew. When my previous ways of soothing myself through sleepless nights did not work. When the rocking and imaginary friend or real Spirit could not tell me, "Baby, it's going to be okay." When the verbal "shhhs" I made as I visualized the comforting scene only led to shorter breaths, I knew. I knew what had died.

A new image appeared.

Cycling. My feet clipped into the pedals, feeling each pull up in my hamstrings, each push down in my quadriceps, creating a circle. Over and over. My palms on the handlebars. The feel of the seat beneath my rear and the way I lift up when I see a bump coming so I won't feel it too harshly. The wind on my cheeks even as I work my way up a hill. My helmet and sunglasses barely perceptible. It's the closest I've come to flight.

And I breathed. Slow and steady. The rushing thoughts of replayed conversations, projected dialogues, things to do, words from books, who really loves me or not, the things that had been swirling in my mind—they cleared.

Whoosh, whoosh.

Breathe, breathe.

I was on the bike.

It was not new to feel as though cycling restored my humanity. I often heard the voice of God while turning the corner on a trail or whisking down a hill at more than twenty-five miles an hour, or going up a hill for five to six miles straight.

But this image at night was new. It was a new way of self-soothing. I had learned how to contain myself, how to hold myself together when I felt I was falling apart. But that didn't work anymore. Now I released myself to the wind.

An image of comfort morphed into an image of freedom.

The biblical verse that my depressive self has long eschewed suddenly made sense:

> They that wait upon God shall renew their strength;
> they shall mount up with wings as eagles.
> (Isaiah 40:31)

Again God appeared renewing my strength: as I spoke with my friend, as I tried to rock myself to sleep, on my bicycle.

And instead of feeling as if I were falling, I felt as if I were being uplifted.

American singer Josh Groban sings it well:

> *When I am down, and oh my soul, so weary;*
> *When troubles come and my heart burdened be*
> *Then I am still and wait here in the silence . . .*
> *You raise me up*

∿

Exploration
How does God renew your strength?

Reflection
What raises you up when you feel low?

epilogue

why resurrection matters

Around Easter time, I'm often asked questions that are particularly pertinent to many Christians, especially around that time of the church calendar:

Do you believe in the bodily resurrection of Christ?

My flippant, every-day-spiritual-life answer is: Does it really matter? Really?!

My scholarly answer is: After reading the late religious scholar Nancy Eiesland's *The Disabled God,* how could I not? Eiesland argues that the physically disabled body of the resurrected Christ (you know, wounded hands and feet) can be a really important touchstone and ministry for individuals who live with physical disabilities. She removes the focus from the empty cross and the tomb to the road to Emmaus. Amazing theological stuff there!

But yes, resurrection does matter—and this is why:

For those of us who live regularly or periodically with the threat of death, life matters.

A lot.

I am one, and I know others, who live many everyday moments closer to death than most people around us might imagine. The possibility of death is not far away. This is no philosophical lament about the finitude implicit in human mortality. Rather, it is the sometimes frightening and disturbingly ordinary texture of our lives.

That death looms near is sometimes a product of our social and economic and geographical and age-related realities. We see loved ones and strangers around us transitioning both peacefully or with great resistance to the space beyond life. Other times, the threat of death is an unfortunate-though-known consequence of the decisions that we make as we take stances for justice, love, inclusion, humanity, and earth.

And there are the instances when the threat of death comes from within. When death can seem a welcome respite from the weariness of trying to subsist in the midst of desperation. When the loss of community, family, and sense of self comes faster and easier than the tenacity to hold onto and build community, family, and soul. Yes, I'm talking about suicide here.

As a theologian, I can't express how important it is to distinguish these different kinds of living-in-the-midst-of-death when referring to what happens to Jesus on the cross. Yet as a person who strives to live out my faith every day—hey, as a person who strives to live from day to day—I simply say that for those of us who have known metaphorical and literal death, not once, not twice, but more times that we can count, resurrection matters.

To be able to find life when one cannot see even an arm's length in front of oneself, and to be able to feel or know love and breath after life has been vitiated, is nothing short of a miracle.

To see value in the past after seasons of hopeless desperation and to stay in community when all reason says to walk away is how I know mercy.

To break bread with people who have intentionally hurt you and to retell stories that have lost meaning in the face of the apathy and hopelessness invoked by looking around is how I think of grace.

And the mystery is not that some people cannot do this; the mystery is that any of us manage to.

Resurrection reminds us what my friends of faith and I know so clearly: that finding life after death and even perseverance in the face of death is divine activity.

Our wills and fortitudes alone shrivel when confronted with the task.

And even if our God is not personal or loving, or transcendent or speaking to us, something outside of us and greater than us and yet deeply within us moves us individually and communally to cling to the life side of the cliff.

For me, this is the message and hope and value and reminder of the resurrection: that it is God that maintains hope amidst death.

And while I do not find it salvific in any classical sense, it is the hope that fuels my daily journey and has, thus far, kept me on this side of the rock. I dare not call that salvation, but it is nothing small either.

Many years, my current state of mind and spirit is closer to Maundy Thursday and Good Friday than Resurrection Sunday. I know what it means to be closer to Saturday night than Sunday morning. These devotions become words to remind and encourage myself.

Even for a minister and scholar and questioning person of faith like myself, resurrection matters. Resurrection is everything.

sources

day 3

Layli Phillips, "Womanism: On Its Own," in *The Womanist Reader*, ed. Layli Phillips (New York: Routledge, 2006), xxxiii.

day 4

James Cone, *The Spirituals and the Blues* (1972; repr., Maryknoll, NY: Orbis, 1992), 6.

day 5

C. S. Lewis, *Mere Christianity* (1952; repr., New York: HarperOne, 1980), 140.

day 6

M. Scott Peck, *The Road Less Traveled: A New Psychology of Love, Traditional Values and Spiritual Growth*, 25th Anniversary ed. (New York: Touchstone, 2003), 15, 19.

day 7

Zora Neale Hurston, *Their Eyes Were Watching God* (1937; repr., New York: Harper Perennial, 2010), 85.

day 10

Friedrich Nietzsche, "Twilight of the Idols," in *The Portable Nietzsche*, ed. and trans. Walter Kaufmann (1954; repr., New York: Penguin Books, 1976), 467.

day 18

Paul Tillich, *Dynamics of Faith* (1957; repr., New York: Perennial, 2001), 25.

Andrew Solomon, *The Noonday Demon: An Atlas of Depression* (New York: Touchstone, 2002).

Nancy L. Eiesland, *The Disabled God: Toward a Liberatory Theology of Disability* (Nashville: Abingdon Press, 1994).

day 21

Herman Hesse, *Siddhartha* (1922; repr., Boston: Shambala, 2000), 146.

day 22

Anne Lamott, *Plan B: Further Thoughts on Faith* (New York: Riverhead, 2006), 66.

day 23

Eric Bazilian, "One of Us," performed by Joan Osborne on *Relish*, Island/Mercury, 1995.

day 24

Cheryl Townsend Gilkes, "The Black Church as a Therapeutic Community: Suggested Areas for Research into the Black Religious Experience," *Journal of the Interdenominational Theological Center* 8, no. 1 (Fall 1980): 38.

day 30

Henri Nouwen, "A Spirituality of Waiting: Being Alert to God's Presence in Our Lives," *Weavings* 2, no. 1 (Jan.–Feb. 1987).

acknowledgments

There are so many people who supported me in the process of blogging and writing this book.

I received financial support from the Lilly Research Expense Grant administered by the Association of Theological Schools and from the Career Enhancement Fellowship for Junior Faculty of the Woodrow Wilson National Fellowship Foundation.

I appreciate Miguel de la Torre, who gave me the right motivation at the right time to transform an academic project into one that is more accessible and, honestly, more meaningful to me. Thank you to C. Yvonne Augustine for her editorial assistance. Jim Palmer and Bruce G. Epperly, inspiring spiritual writers, were helpful with their comments on early drafts. Maxine B. Cunningham and Pauline A. Bigby, you are my longest and greatest supporters. Beth Wright at Trio Bookworks has been a capable and encouraging editor. Thank you, David Lott. Jeff Obafemi Carr encouraged me in the details of making this book actually happen.

To everyone who read the blog, shared it, and emailed me with your story, your acts encourage me more than you can know. And to those who walk so much of this way with me— Melissa Johnston, Kai Jackson-Issa, Connie Tuttle, Andre Myers,

Jesse Harris Bathrick, Jan Collins-Eaglin, Mark Whitlock, and my life's partner, Michael Datcher— you are the ones who see and hear. Thank you.

about the author

Monica A. Coleman is a writer, scholar, and activist. She is an ordained minister in the African Methodist Episcopal (AME) Church. She has received degrees from Harvard, Vanderbilt, and Claremont Graduate universities. She is currently Associate Professor of Constructive Theology and African American Religions at Claremont School of Theology in the Claremont Lincoln University consortium in Southern California. She is the author of *The Dinah Project* and *Making a Way Out of No Way* and the coeditor of *Creating Women's Theology*. She is also the editor of the forthcoming volume *Ain't I a Womanist Too? Third Wave Womanist Religious Thought*.

She blogs on depression and faith at www.BeautifulMindBlog .com. Her work on depression and faith has been featured on the Huffington Post, Beliefnet.com, and PsychCentral.com. She is also a regular contributor on Patheos.com. Dr. Coleman is committed to connecting faith and social justice and speaks regularly throughout the United States on sexual violence, domestic violence, mental health, and theology.

CPSIA information can be obtained at www.ICGtesting.com
Printed in the USA
BVOW070957040613

322402BV00002B/17/P

9 780985 140205